ISBN 978-0-365-13005-5
PIBN 11267168

MANITOBA

CONTAINING

1. The names of the Post Offices alphabetically arranged.
2. Showing the distribution of the different post offices from a standpoint east of Fort William (See page 2).

3. The names of the Postal Car Routes, Sections of Postal Car Routes or Distributing Offices through which matter for the several offices should pass.

4. The names of the Offices to which the matter is forwarded by the Railway Mail Clerks or Distributing Offices when not mailed direct. (Direct Mails are indicated by dotted lines).

5. The names of the Mail Routes by which the offices are served when not situated on a line of Railway. When ·ffice is served by two or more routes the hours of departure from the several terminal points : ·n.

INSTRUCTIONS.

1. Matter for any Office which is supplied by more than one route should be forwarded by the one by which it will m ι speedily reach its destination.

2. When any doubt exists as to the proper Railway route by which matter should be forwarded, application should be made to the Superintendent, Railway Mail Service. Similar information should be obtained from the Post Office Inspector regarding Mail Routes off the line of Railway.

3. Offices ne~·ly established, and Offices to which new names have been given, should be written in the List of Offices naving the same initial letter. To the entries under each letter should be prefixed consecutive numbers, which numbers should be neatly inserted in their places in the General List, in whic the names of the new Offices or the new names of the old Offices should, in proper order, appear. The numbering should be from one upwards in each letter.

4. In case of change of name, the old name should be erased from the list and *"changed to*........ ...." the new name) written opposite to the erasure. Opposite the entry of the new name should be written ("formerly... ...." (the old name.)

5. It is the duty of Superintendents of Railway Mail Service and Postmasters *personally* to see that the Distribution Books furnished to each Clerk under their supervision are corrected from the Lists issued from the Post Office Department and the Office of the Controller R.M.S. at Ottawa.

POST OFFICE DEPARTMENT,
    OFFICE OF CONTROLLER R.M.S.
        OTTAWA, March 25th, 1914.

KEY TO EAST OF FORT WILLIAM STANDPOINT SCHEME

1. W. & M.J.R.P.O.	8. Winnipeg Dis.	15e. Saskatoon Dis.
1a. Portage la Prairie Dis.	8a. Ft. F. & W. R.P.O.	16. N. P. & M.J.R.P.O.
1b. Macgregor & Dis.	8b. Selkirk & Dis.	16a. Wey & Leth. R.P.O.
1c. Carberry & Dis.	8c. Stonewall & Dis.	17. M. J. & C. R.P.O.
1d. Virden & Dis.	8d. E. & W. R.P.O.	17a. Maple Creek & Dis.
1e. Moosomin & Dis.	8e. B. L. & W.R.P.O.	17b. Swift Current Dis.
1f. Qu'Appelle Dis.	8f. G. & W.R.P.O.	17c. Calgary.
1g. Regina Dis.	9. B. & E. R.P.O.	18. M.H. & N.R.P.O.
1h. Moose Jaw Dis.	9a. B. & R. R.P.O.	18a. Lethbridge Dis.
2. W. & *Kam* P. O.	10. Brandon Dis.	18b. Edmonton City.
2a. Dauphin Dis.	11. S. & R. R.P.O.	19. Mac. & Cal. R.P.O.
2b. Gilbert Plains Dis.	11a. R. & W. R.P.O.	20. C. & E. R.P.O.
2c. Grand View Dis.	11b. Maryfield—Radville.	20a. Ed & Mirror.
2d. Humboldt Dis.	12. W. & P.A.R.P.O. No. 1.	21. Edmonton Dis.
3. W. & Y. R.P.O.	12a. W. & P.A.R.P.O. No. 2.	21a. Wpg. & Rivers R.P.O.
3a. East of Portage la P.	12b. Swan River & Dis.	22. Riv. & Wain. E. of Sask.
3b. Neepawa Dis.	13. B. & S. R.P.O. No. 1.	22a. Riv. & Wain.West of Sask.
3c. Russell Dis.	13a. B. & S. R.P.O. No. 2.	22b. Wain. & Ed. R.P.O.
3d. Y. & S. R.P.O.		23. Reg. & Out. R.P.O.
3e. Saltcoats Dis.	14. H. & E. R.P.O.	24. S. & H. R.P.O.
4. W. & V. R.P.O.	14a. Battleford Dis.	24a. Macklin Dis.
5. W. & S. R.P.O.	14b. No. Battleford Dis.	24b. Reg. & Melville, R.P.O.
5a. Carman & Dis.	14c. Hard & Wet. R.P.O.	25. B. V. & Veg. R.P.O.
6. W. & N. R.P.O.	14d. C. & L.R.P.O.	26. D. & B. V.R.P.O.
6a. Morden & Dis.	15. R. & P.A. No. 1.	27. Van & S. C. R.P. O.
6b. Boissevain & Dis.	15a. R. & P.A. No. 2.	28. S. C. & Prussia. R.P.O.
7. Ft. Win. & W.R.P.O.	15b. S. & A. R.P.O.	29. Out & Mack. R.P.O.
	15d. Prince Albert Dis.	30. Ed. & Edson. R.P.O.

SCHEDULE showing names of Railways from which Post Offices in Manitoba are served; the terminal points of the several Postal Car routes, or sections of Postal Car routes on these Railways, and the abbreviations by which these terminal points are designated in the following Distribution List; (The names of Railway Post Offices are given in all cases from East to West and from South to North).

Abbreviations In Distribution List.	Name of Railway.	Terminal Routes between which Postal Cars run.
B. & E.	Canadian Pacific Ry	Brandon......Estevan
B. & R.	Canadian Northern Ry	Brandon.......Regina
B. L. & W.	Canadian Pacific Ry	Boundary Line. Winnipeg
B. & S.	" "	Brandon.......Saskatoon
E. & W.	Great Northern Ry	Emerson ....Winnipeg
Ft. F. & W.	Canadian Northern Ry	Fort Frances...Winnipeg.
Ft. W. & W.	Canadian Pacific Ry	Fort William...Winnipeg
G. & W.	" "	Gretna........Winnipeg
Pem. & Wpg	Northern Pacific Ry	Pembina, N.D.Winnipeg
R. & W.	Canadian Pacific Ry	Reston........Wolseley
Riv. & Wain	Grand Trunk Pacific Ry	Rivers........Wainwright
S. & R.	Canadian Pacific Ry	Souris.........Regina
W. & H.	Canadian Northern Ry	Winnipeg......Humboldt
W. & M. J.	Canadian Pacific Ry	Winnipeg......Moose Jaw
W. & N.	" " " "	Winnipeg,......Napinka
W. & P. A.	Canadian Northern Ry	Winnipeg :....Prince Albert
W. & R.	Grand Trunk Pacific Ry	Winnipeg......Rivers
W. & S.	Canadian Pacific Ry	Winnipeg......Souris
W. & V.	Canadian Northern Ry	Winnipeg......Virden
W. & Y.	Canadian Pacific Ry	Winnipeg......Yorkton

59103—1½

Office	Key No.	County	Distribution		
~~[illegible]~~	~~S.~~	~~[illegible]~~		~~Chaplin~~	~~[illegible] 8-00~~

MANITOBA DISTRIBUTION LIST

The first column under the Head "Distribution" shows the Postal Car Route or Distributing Office through which matter for the several Offices should pass. R.P.O. Routes making exhange of mails are given first. B. Car services and Stage Services follow. The second column under the head "Distribution" shows the Office on which the matter is forwarded by the Railway Clerk or Distributing Office when not mailed direct. The third column gives the frequency and other necessary particulars regarding the service. Dy.* means daily including Sunday. Dy. means daily except Sunday. The letters (S.) & (W.) following the name of the forward Office show how the matter should be forwarded in Summer and Winter respectively. A* before the name of an Office, indicates a Customs Port or Out port, and (S.) after the name of an Office indicates a Summer Office.

OFFICE	KEY No.	COUNTY	DISTRIBUTION		
Abbeville.........	8	Dauphin.......	Winnipeg......	Deer Horn.....	Mon. Fri. 14.45.
Abigail...........	6b	Souris.........	{W. & N..... / Brandon.....}	Boissevain.....	Sat. 8.30.
Acorn............	10	Brandon......	Brandon..........................		Dy. Tr. 196.
Addingham........	3	P. la Prairie...	W. & Y.... Portage La Prairie Langruth	Westbourne....	Fri. 7.00.
Agardsley.........	2	Dauphin.......	W. & H. Kam.	Glenella......	{ Bellhampton / Sat. 12.00. }
Alexander.........	1	Brandon.......	{W. & M. J.... / B. & S......}		{ Dy. trs. 53, 54. / Dy.*tr. 3, 4. / Dy. trs. 59, 60. }
Allanlea..........	2	Dauphin.......	W. & H. Kam.	Glenella.......	Sat. 12.30.
Almasippi...... ..	4	Macdonald.....	W. & V........	Graysville.....	Mon. Fri. 13.00.
Alpine...........	12b	Dauphin.......	W. & P.A. S.R.	Swan River....	Benito, Tue. Sat. 13.00.
Altamont.........	8	Macdonald.....	Winnipeg.......		Dy. tr. 15, C.N.R.
Altona...........	8f	Lisgar.........	G. & W........		Dy. trs. 123, 124.
Amaranth.........	3	Dauphin.......	W. & Y. Portage La Prairie Langruth	Westbourne....	Hollywood, Sat. 13.00.
Angusville........	3b	Marquette.....	{W. & Y...... / S.R. / W. & P.A.....}	{Neepawa..... / Russell....... / Neepawa...... }	M. W. F. tr. 17 C.N.R. / T. T. S. tr. 18 C.N.R. / M. W. F. tr. 17 C.N.R.
Arawana..........	1	Brandon.......	W. & M. J.....	Elkhorn.......	Fri. 13.00.
Arbakka..........	8e	Provencher....	{E. & W...... / B. L. & W.....}	Emerson......	Vita. Tue. Sat. 9.30.
Arborg...........	8	Selkirk........	Winnipeg.......		Dy. tr. 207.
Arden............	3	P. la Prairie....	W. & Y........		Dy. trs. 57, 58.

OFFICE	KEY No.	COUNTY	DISTRIBUTION
		Winnipeg	

OFFICE	KEY No.	COUNTY.	DISTRIBUTION		
Argyle..............	8	Macdonald......	Winnipeg.......	Warrenton.....	M. W. F. 11.00.
Argyle Station.......	8	Selkirk........	Winnipeg.......	....	M. W. F. tr. 129.
Arnaud............	8e	Provencher.....	B. L. & W......	....	Dy. trs. 109, 110.
Arnes.............	8	Selkirk........	Winnipeg........	~~Gimli~~........	M. Fri. ~~8.00.~~ *mod* $\hbar$ *no 235*
Arrow River.......	10	Marquette......	Brandon.......	....	Dy. tr. 135. C.P.R.
Assessippi........	3c	Marquette.....	W. & Y........	Russell........	Tu. Fri. 13.30.
Ashern...........	8	Dauphin.......	Winnipeg......	....	M. W. F. tr. 9.
Ashville..........	2	Dauphin.......	W. & ~~H~~ *jen*..	....	M. W. F. trs. 1, 2.
Atwell............	8	Macdonald.....	Winnipeg.......	Warrenton.....	M. W. F. 12.30.
Aubigny...........	8	Provencher.....	Winnipeg......	....	M. W. F. tr. 15.
Austin............	1	P. la Prairie....	W. & M. J.....	....	Dy. trs. 53, 54.
Aweme.'..........	5	P. la Prairie....	W. & S........	Treesbank.....	Fri. 14.15.

Office	Key No.	County	Distribution
Beaman	m	wpeg	Louise Bridge	Ex Sens 10.15
Beckville		Portage Laprairie Amaranth	Fr. 8.00
Berens River			
Barrier Lake		K & NB, Quill Lake	Tri, 8.th

OFFICE	KEY No.	COUNTY	DISTRIBUTION		
Badger............	8a	Provencher....	Ft. F. & W.		M. W. F. Sat. tr. 22.
Bagot.............	1	P. la Prairie....	W. & M. J.....	....	Dy. trs. 53, 54.
Baldur............	4	Souris...........	W. & V.........	....	Dy. trs. 11, 12.
Balmoral..........	8	Selkirk........	Winnipeg.......	....	Dy. tr. 107 C.P.R.
Balsam Bay........	8	Selkirk........	Winnipeg.......	East Selkirk.....	Sat. 7.00.
*Bannerman.......	6b	Brandon........	{ W. & N...... Brandon...... }	Boissevain....	Dy. tr. 196. G. N. R.
Bardal............	11a	Brandon........	R. & W........	Ebor...........	Fri. 13.00.
Barnsley..........	5a	Macdonald....	{ W. & V. W. & S. }	Carman.......	M. W. F. tr. 238, C.P.R.
Barrows...........	12a	Keewatin......	W. & P. A.	....	Dy. trs. 3, 4.
Basswood.........	3	Marquette.....	W. & Y........	....	Dy. trs. 57, 58.
Bayton...........	8	Dauphin.......	Winnipeg.......	Moose Horn....	Tue. 13.30.
Beaconsfield......	5	Macdonald.....	W. & S........	Treherne......	Mon. Fri. 13.15.
Beausejour........	8	Selkirk........	Winnipeg......	....	Dy. tr. 112, C.P.R.
Beaver...........	12	P. la Prairie...	W. & P. A. (1).	....	Dy. trs. 3, 4.
Beckville.........	3	Dauphin.......	W. & Y........	Westbourne....	Fri. 7.00.
Bedford Station....	8a	Provencher....	Ft. F. & W.		Dy. tr. 22
Belcourt..........	3a	Macdonald.....	W. & Y. (1)....	Poplar Point...	Tu. Fri. 10.15.
Belleview.........	4	Souris..........	W. & V........	....	Dy. trs. 11, 12.
Belhampton......	2	Dauphin.......	W. & R..........	Glenella.......	Fri. 14.00.
Belmont..........	4	Souris..........	{ W. & V...... Brandon...... }	....	Dy. trs. 11, 12. Dy. tr. 114 C.N.R.
Benard...........	12	Macdonald.....	W. & P. A. (1).	....	Dy. tr. 3.
Bender Hamlet.....	8	Selkirk	Winnipeg......	Inwood........	Sat. 8.00.
Benito............	12b	Dauphin.......	W. & P. A.	Swan River....	T. T. S. tr. 142 C. N. R.
Berens River......	8	Selkirk........	Winnipeg....	{ Selkirk....... Icelandic River }	(S) By Boat semi weekly. (W) Icelandic Riv. 2nd Sat. 9.00.
Beresford.........	10	Brandon.......	{ Brandon...... W. & S..... B. & E..... S. & R..... }	Souris.........	Dy. tr. 137, C.P.R. Dy. Tr. 138, C.P.R.
Berlo.............	8	Selkirk........	Winnipeg......	Meleb.........	Fri. 13.00.
Bernice...........	6	Souris..........	{ W. & N...... B. & E...... }	Napinka.......	Tu.-Sat. 11.00.

OFFICE	KEY No.	COUNTY	DISTRIBUTION		
Big Woody	Man.	N. & P.A.	Swan River		Sat. 14.30
Birdtail		6 & S. B.	Neepawa.		m w f to 17
Bodham		W. & S.R.	Ethelbert		Sat 15.00
Blackdale	U. Municipal		Emsville		Tue, Fri. 16.45.

OFFICE	KEY No.	COUNTY	DISTRIBUTION		
Berton............	12	P. la Prairie....	W. & P. A.	....	Dy. tr. 3.
Bethany..........	3b	Marquette	{W. & Y...... W. & S.R. ...}	Neepawa......	M. W. F. tr. 17, C.N.R.
Beulah............	12	Marquette.....	{W. & B.A. (1) Brandon..... W. & Y......	.... Miniota...... Birtle.........	M. W. F. tr. 3. T. T. S. 8.00. M. W. S. 12.00.
Bield.............	2	Marquette.....	W. & Kam	....	Dy. tr. 1.
Bifrost............	8	Selkirk........	Winnipeg.......	{Arborg....... Icelandic Rive	Mon. Fri. 14.00. Tue. Sat. 8.00.
Binscarth.........	3	Marquette....	W. & Y......	....	Dy. trs. 57, 58.
Birch River...,....	12a	Dauphin.......	& P. A......	....	Dy. tr. 3.
Bird River........	8	Selkirk........	{Winnipeg.... F. W. & W.....	.... Molson.......	Lac du Bonnet. Wed. 8.00. Fri. 14.00.
Bird's Hill........	8	Selkirk........	Winnipeg......	....	Dy. tr. 112. C.P.R.
Birnie.............	12	Macdonald.....	W. & S.R. (1)...	....	Dy. trs. 3, 4.
Birtle.............	3	Marquette.....	W. & Y......	Amaranth	Dy. trs. 57, 58.
Bluff Creek.......	3	Dauphin.......	W. & Y......	Westbourne....	N. TH. 15.00
*Boissevain.......	6	Souris.........	{W. & N...... Brandon.....	....	Dy. trs. 121, 122. Dy. tr. 196. G.N.R.
Bonnie Doon......	3a	Macdonald.....	W. &. Y. (1)...	Reaburn.......	Tu. Fri. 11.00.
Boultonville.......	6a	Lisgar.........	W. & N.......	Morden.......	Tu. Fri. 8.00.
Bouville..,........	8	Dauphin......	Winnipeg.....	Arborg........	Thu. 16.00.
Bowsman River....	12a	Dauphin......	& P. A......	....	Dy. trs. 3, 4.
Bradwardine.......	10	Brandon.......	Brandon.......	....	Dy. tr. 215, C. P.R.
*Brandon..........	10	Brandon.:....	{W. & M. J..... B. & S...... B. & E...... Winnipeg..... B. & R.......	....	{Dy.* trs. 3, 4, 61, 62. Dy. trs. 53, 54. Dy. tr. 60. Dy. tr. 138. Dy. tr. 101 C.P.R. Dy. tr. 6.
Brandon Hills.....	10	Brandon.......	Brandon.......	....	T. S. tr. 114 C. N. R.
Brewsterville.......	8	Dauphin.......	Winnipeg......	Deer Horn Eriksdale.....	Mon. Fri. 15.00.
Bridge Creek.......	3	P. la Prairie...	W. & Y........	Franklin.......	Tue. Fri. 8.00.
Brierwood.........	1	Brandon.......	W. & M. J.....	Griswold.......	Tu. Fri. 13.30.
Brightstone........	8	Selkirk........	{Winnipeg..... F. W. & W....	.... Molson........	Lac du Bonnet, Fri. 14.00.
Broad Valley.......	8	Dauphin.......	Winnipeg......	Arborg........	Thu. 16.00.
Brokenhead........	8	Selkirk........	Winnipeg......	Beausejour.....	Fri. 14.00.

1 Closed via Brandon 1-12-14

OFFICE	KEY No.	COUNTY	DISTRIBUTION		

OFFICE	KEY No.	COUNTY.			DISTRIBUTION	
Brookdale.........	1b	P. la Prairie...	W. & M. J.....	Macgregor.....	M. W. F. tr. 219, C.P.R.	
Broomhill.........	9	Souris.........	B. & E.......	Melita....		
Brown.............	6a	Lisgar.........	W. & N......	Morden.........	Tu. Fri. 14.00.	
Bru..............	5	Souris.........	W. & S.......	Cypress River..	M. W. F. 14.30.	
Brunkild..........	4	Macdonald.....	W. & V. (1)....	....	Dy. tr. 11, C.N.R.	
Bruxelles.........	5	Macdonald.....	W. & S.......	Holland.......	M. W. F. Sat. 14.20.	
Bunclody.........	10	Souris.........	Brandon......	....	Dy. tr. 196, G.N.R.	
Burnbank.........	1	Marquette.....	W. & M. J.....	Elkhorn......	Tu. Fri. 8.00.	
Burnside..........	1	P. la Prairie....	W. & M. J.....	....	Dy. trs. 53, 54.	
Butler Station......	9a	Brandon.......	B. & R........	....	Dy. tr. 6, C.N.R.	

1 Bru closed send to Cypress River 1.2.16.

OFFICE	KEY No.	COUNTY		DISTRIBUTION
(1) Cameron Island, Ont., *Ste. dupy*				{ Ingolf (wual) Tue. 8.00 Kenora (S) Mon & Thur.
Clematis		Dauphin	Winnipeg	Inwood St Adelard Sat 10.3

(1) Closed send mail 8 Kautka.

Office	Key No.	County.		Distribution		
Caliento...........	8e	Provencher.....	E. & W...... B. L. & W...	Emerson.......	Dy. tr. 106.	
Cameron...........	6	Souris.........	W. & N...... Deloraine.....	....	Dy. tr. 121 via 139, 271. Dy. trs. 139, 271, C.P.R.	
Camper...........	8	Dauphin.......	Winnipeg......	....	M. W. F. tr. 9.	
·Camperville.......	12	Marquette....	W. & A. *Dauphin*	Winnipegosis....	Tue. 8.00.	
*Carberry...........	1c	P. la Prairie....	W. & M.J..... Winnipeg..... Neepawa.....	....	Dy. trs. 53, 54. Dy.* trs. 3, 4. Dy. tr. 101, C.P.R. T. T. S. tr. 116 C.N.R.	
Cardale...........	12	Marquette.....	W. & A.......	....	M. W. F. tr. 3.	
			W. & Y.......	Neepawa......	M. W. F. tr. 131.	
Cardinal..........	4	Macdonald.....	W. & V.......	....	Dy. trs. 11, 12.	
Carey.............	8e	Provencher.....	B. L. & W.....	....	Dy. tr. 110.	
Carlowrie.........	8e	Provencher.....	B. L. & W.....	Arnaud........	Fri. 9.00.	
Carman...........	5a	Macdonald.....	W. & V....... W. & S.......	....	Dy. trs. 11, 12. Dy. tr. 55 via 237 C.P.R.	
Carnegie..........	10	Brandon.......	Brandon.......	....	Dy. tr. 259, C.P.R.	
Carroll...........	5	Brandon.......	W. & S.......	....	Dy. trs. 55, 56.	
Cartwright........	6	Souris.........	W. & N......	....	Dy. trs. 121, 122.	
Cayer.............	8	Dauphin.......	Winnipeg......	Mulvihill......	Reykjavik. Mon. 15.00.	
Cedar Lake.......	12a	Keewatin......	W. & P. A.....	Hudson Bay Jct	....Le Pas, Monthly.	
Charleswood......	8	Macdonald.....	Winnipeg.....	....	M. W. F. 15.15.	
Chater...........	1	Brandon.......	W. & M. J.....	....	Dy. trs. 53. 54.	
Chatfield.........	8	Dauphin.......	Winnipeg......	Inwood........	Bender Hamlet Sat. 13.00	
Chortitz..........	8a	Provencher.....	Ft. F. & W....	Steinbach......	Mon. Fri. 7.45.	
Clandeboye........	8	Selkirk........	Winnipeg......	....	Dy. tr. 235. C.P.R.	
Clan William......	3b	Marquette.....	W. & Y...... W. & ...	Neepawa......	M.W.F. tr. 17, C.N.R.	
Clarkleigh.........	8	Dauphin.......	Winnipeg.....	....	Mon. Wed. Fri. tr. 9.	
Clear Springs......	8 a	Provencher.....	Ft. F. & W....	....	Dy. tr. 22.	
Clearwater........	6	Lisgar.........	W. & N.......	....	Dy. trs. 121. 122.	
Cloverleaf........	8	Selkirk........	Winnipeg......	....	Dy. tr. 2. C.P.R.	
Coatstone..........	6	Souris.........	W. & N.......	Deloraine......	T.T.S. 10.00.	

OFFICE	KEY No.	COUNTY	DISTRIBUTION		
Cowan			W , *S. R.* ~~P.O.~~		Ev Sun to 3
Craigsford			W , *S. R.* ~~P.O.~~	Bowsman River	W , S. 11, 00

OFFICE	KEY No.	COUNTY	DISTRIBUTION		
Colcleugh..........	8	Dauphin.......	Winnipeg......	Ashern........	Sat. 7.00.
Cold Springs.......	8	Dauphin.......	Winnipeg......	Oak Point.....	Lundar Tue. Sat. 9.00.
Cook's Creek......	8	Selkirk.......	Winnipeg......	Oak Bank.....	T.T.S. 9.45.
Copley............	6	Souris........	W. & N........	Lyleton........	Sat. 15.45.
			W. & E.	....	M. W. F. tr. 3.
Cordova...........	12	Marquette.....	W. & M. J....	Macgregor.....	Moorepark. Tu. Fri. 11.00.
			W. & Y.......	Neepawa......	M. W. F. tr. 131.
Coulter............	6	Souris........	W. & N......	....	Dy. tr. 121, via 139, 271 C.P.R.
			Deloraine.....	....	Dy. trs. 139, 271.
Coultervale........	6	Souris........	W. & N.......	Coulter........	Tu. Sat. 16. 30.
Cowdery...........	8	Dauphin.......	Winnipeg......	Eriksdale......	Mon. Fri. 15.00.
Crandell...........	10	Marquette.....	Brandon.......	....	Dy. tr. 135, C.P.R.
Creeford,..........	1	Brandon.......	W. & M. J....	Douglas St'n...	Mon. Wed. Fri. 8.30.
Crescent...........	11	Souris........	S. & R.......	Sinclair St'n...	Tu. Thu. Sat. 15.00.
Crewe.............	3	Marquette.....	W. & Y.......	Foxwarren.....	Mon. Thur. 10.45.
Cromer Station.....	9a	Brandon.......	B. & R.......	....	Dy. trs. 5, 6, C.N.R.
Cromwell..........	8	Selkirk.......	Winnipeg......	Beausejour.....	Fri. 14.00.
*Crystal City.......	6	Lisgar........	W. & N......	....	Dy. trs. 121, 122.
Cutross...........	5	Macdonald.....	W. & S. (1)...	....	Dy. trs. 55, 56.
Cypress River......	5	Macdonald.....	W. & S........	....	Dy. trs. 55, 56.

1 Changed to Cromer 1/9/15
2 Closed via Foxwarren 1/9/15

Office	Key No.	County	Distribution	
Dand			{B. East, W. Division} Hartney	m.w. Sat 10:30
{Service discontinued (1-9-13)} Delta Stn (S ①)			Portage la Prairie	T.T.S.
Dallas			winnipeg Arborg	Tue 7:00
Davis Point	m	wpeg	St Martins Stn	F... 11.
O nfed	m	ˮ	dnwood Chatfield	Sat ...
Dearlock	Ont.	47, W-	Barwick - Black Hawk	Tue 9:45
Dolly Bay	M.	Winnipeg	Ashern - Golbrum	Sat 14:00

OFFICE	KEY No.	COUNTY	DISTRIBUTION		
Dacotah.........	8	Macdonald.....	W. & P. A. (1). *S. R.*	....	Dy. tr. 3.
Dallas............	8	Dauphin.......	Winnipeg......	Arborg........	Vidir. Tue. 13.00.
Daly.............	1d	Brandon.......	{W. & M. J... {W. & V..... }	Virden.........	Fri. 17.00.
Danvers..........	3b	Marquette.....	{W. & Y...... {W. & P. S. R. }	Neepawa......	Erickson, Mon. Fri. **17.15**
Darlingford........	6	Lisgar........	W. & N......	....	Dy. trs. 121, 122.
*Dauphin.........	2a	Dauphin.......	{W. & ‡ *Kam.* {W. & P. S. R. }	....	Dy. trs. 1, 2. Dy. trs. 3, 4.
Decker............	12	Marquette.....	{W. & P. A. {W & Y...... }	Neepawa......	M. W. F. tr. 3. M. W. F. tr. 131.
Deepdale..........	2	Marquette.....	W. & ‡ *Kam.*	....	Dy.* trs. 1, 2.
Deer Horn........	8	Dauphin......	Winnipeg......	....	Mon., Wed., Fri. tr. 9.
Deerwood.........	4	Macdonald.....	W. & V.......	Somerset.......	M. W. F. tr. 16, C.N.R.
Deleau...........	5	Brandon.......	S. & R. (1).....	....	Dy. trs. 55, 56.
*Deloraine........	6	Souris.........	W. & N......	....	Dy. trs. 121, 122.
Dennis Lake......	8	Selkirk........	Winnipeg......	Inwood........	Sat. 12.00.
Derry............	8	Selkirk........	Winnipeg........	....	M. W. F. 17.00.
Desford...........	6b	Souris.........	{Brandon...... {W. & N...... Boissevain....}		Dy. tr. 196, G.N.R.
De Wet...........	6	Provencher.....	W. & N......	....	Dy. trs. 121, 122.
Dickens..........	8	Macdonald.....	Winnipeg......	....	Dy. 7.30.
Dnieper..........	2a	Dauphin.......	Dauphin......	....	Wed. Fri. tr. 137.
Dog Creek........	8	Dauphin.......	Winnipeg......	Mulvihill......	Tue. 9.00. Fri. 16.00.
Dominion City....	8e	Provencher.....	B. L. & W.....	....	Dy. trs. 109, 110.
Douglas Station....	1	Brandon.......	W. & M. J.....	....	Dy. trs. 53, 54.
Drifting River......	2b	Dauphin.......	W. & ‡ *Kam.*	Gilbert Plains..	Venlaw, Wed. Sat. 10.15
Dropmore.........	3c	Marquette.....	W. & Y......	Russell........	M. W. F. tr. 17, C.N.R.
Dry River........	4	Souris.........	W. & V......	Mariapolis.....	Tu. Fri. 15.00.
Dublin Bay.......	12	Dauphin.......	W. & P. A. *S. R.*	Sifton.........	Sat. 13.00.
Duck Mountain....	2	Marquette.....	W. & ‡ *Kam.*	Togo..........	Fri. 13.00.
Dufresne..........	8a	Provencher.....	R. F. & W. *Ft. H. L.*		M. W. F. tr. 22.
Dufrost...........	8e	Provencher....	B. L. & W.....	....	Dy. tr. 110.
Dugald...........	8	Selkirk........	Winnipeg......	....	M. W. F. tr. 22.

OFFICE	KEY No.	COUNTY	DISTRIBUTION

OFFICE z	KEY No.	COUNTY	DISTRIBUTION		
Dunallan..........	6b	Souris.........	{W. & N.....} {Brandon.....}	Boissevain.....	Tu. Fri. 9.00.
Dundee...........	8	Selkirk........	Winnipeg......	....	Tu. Fri. 7.00.
Dunrea...........	4	Souris.........	W. & V........	....	Dy. trs. 11, 12.
Dunston..........	6a	Lisgar........	W. & N......	Morden........	Tu. Fri. 16.00.
Durban...........	12b	Dauphin.......	W. & P.A.....	Swan River....	T. T. S. tr. 142 C N.R.
Dynevor..........	8b	Selkirk........	Winnipeg......	Selkirk........	Tu. Fri. 8.00.

1 Closed via Morden 1-11-14

Office	Key No.	County			Distribution	
Ellis	Ont	Fort William				M-W. F. To 25
ElkDale		Dauphin	W & Ram	MaRinak	St. Paul du Lac	Sat. 11

OFFICE	KEY No.	COUNTY		DISTRIBUTION	
East Kildonan	8	Selkirk	Winnipeg		Dy. 10.45.
East Bay	12	Dauphin	W. & *Raue.* (1).	Makinak	Tu. Fri. 7.00.
East Selkirk	8	Selkirk	Winnipeg		Dy. tr. 112. C.P.R.
Ebor	11	Brandon	R. & W. (1)		Dy. tr. 245.
Eden	12	Dauphin	W. & (1)		Dy. trs. 3, 4.
Edrans	1b	P. la Prairie	W. & M. J	Macgregor	M. W. F. tr. 219 C.P.R.
Edwards Point	8	Selkirk	Winnipeg	Queen's Valley.	Tu. Fri. 18.00.
Edwin	1a	P. la Prairie	P. la Prairie		Dy. tr. 5, C.N.R.
Elgin	4	Souris	W. & V		Dy. trs. 11, 12.
Elie	12	Macdonald	W. & P. A (1).		Dy. trs. 3, 4.
Elkhorn	1	Brandon	{ W. & M. J		{ Dy.* trs. 3, 4-61-62.
					{ Dy. trs. 53, 54.
			{ B. & S		Dy. trs. 59, 60.
Elk Ranch	12	Dauphin	W. & (1).	Eden	Tue. Fri. 11.00.
Elm Creek	5	Macdonald	W. & S. (1)		Dy. trs, 55, 56.
Elm Grove	8	Provencher	Winnipeg		M. W. F. tr. 22 C.N.R.
Elphinstone	3b	Marquette	{ W. & Y	Neepawa	M. W. F. tr. 17 C.N.R.
			{ W. & P. A		
Elton	1	Brandon	W. & M. J	Douglas St'n	M. W. F. 8.30.
Elva	9	Souris	B. & E		Dy. trs. 137-138
*Emerson	8e	Provencher	{ E. & W		Dy. tr. 8, G. N. R.
			{ B. L. & W		Dy. tr. 110, C.P.R.
Emesville	8	Selkirk	Winnipeg	Middle Church.	M. W. F. 15.30.
Eriksdale	8	Dauphin	Winnipeg		M. W. F. tr. 9.
Erickson	3b	Marquette	{ W. & Y	Neepawa	M. W. F. tr. 17, C.N.R.
			{ W. &		
Erinview	8c	Macdonald	Winnipeg	Stonewall	Thur. 7.30.
Erinview Station	8	Macdonald	Winnipeg		M. W. F. tr. 129.
Ethelbert	12	Dauphin	W. &		Dy. trs. 3, 4.
Ewart	11	Brandon	R. & W. (1)		Dy. tr. 245.

OFFICE	KEY No.	COUNTY	DISTRIBUTION			
Florye			Ft Fis + wpeg	Woodridge		Fri 12.30
Flanders	Ont.	Port Arthur				Dy. ex. tr. 1.
		Ft. Frances				Dy. Tr 2
Fort Garry	M.	Rosenfeld	Winnipeg			
Finmack	Ont.	St Mu. orufy				Dy T. 1.

OFFICE	KEY No.	COUNTY	DISTRIBUTION		
Fairfax............	4	Souris..........	W. & V..........	....	Dy. trs. 11, 12.
Fairford..........	8	Dauphin.......	Winnipeg.......	....	M. W. F. tr. 9.
Fairhall..........	6	Souris..........	W. & N......	Killarney......	Tu. Sat. 8.30.
Fannystelle.......	5	Macdonald.....	W. &. S. (1).....	....	Dy. trs. 55-56.
Findlay...........	11	Brandon.......	S. & R........	....	Dy. trs. 55, 56.
Firdale...........	21a	P. la Prairie....	W. & Riv......	.	Dy. trs. 1, 2.
Fisher Branch......	8	Dauphin.......	Winnipeg.......	Arborg........	Thu. 16.00.
Fisher River......	8	Selkirk........	Winnipeg.......	Arborg........	Vidir, Tue. 13.00.
Fisherton..........	8	Dauphin.......	Winnipeg.......	Arborg........	Thu. 16.00.
Flee Island........	3a	P. la Prairie....	W. & Y. (1)....	High Bluff.....	Wed. & Fri. 12.30.
Foley.............	8	Selkirk........	Winnipeg.......	Winnipeg Beach	Thu. 7.00.
Fork River........	2a	Dauphin.......	{W. & H̶K̶a̶m̶ ꟼu / W. & R̶e̶s̶ S.R}	Dauphin.......	M̶. W̶. F. tr. 137.
Forrest Station.....	10	Brandon.......	Brandon.......	....	Dy. tr. 133, C.P.R.
Ft. Alexander......	7	Selkirk........	{Winnipeg...... / Ft. Wm. & W. Molson........}		}Lac. du Bonnet, **Fri.8.00**
Fort Ellice'.........	3	Marquette.....	W. & Y...... F̶o̶x̶w̶a̶r̶r̶e̶n̶ B̶i̶r̶t̶l̶e̶		T̶u̶.̶ ̶F̶r̶i̶.̶ ̶8̶.̶0̶0̶ Mon, Thur 10³⁰
Fort-Rouge (sub-office)........	......	Winnipeg.......	Winnipeg......	....	City delivery.
Fortier...........	21a	Macdonald.....	W. & Riv......	....	Dy. trs. 1, 2.
Foxwarren.........	3	Marquette.....	W. & Y........	....	Dy. trs. 57, 58.
Framnes..........	8	Selkirk........	Winnipeg.......	Arborg........	Mon. Fri. 13.00.
Franklin..........	3	P. la Prairie....	W. & Y..,	....	Dy. trs. 57, 58.
Freedale..........	1̶2̶	Dauphin.......	W. & P̶.̶ A̶.̶ (1)..	Makinak......	East Bay, Tue. **Fri. 7.00.**

Office	Key No.	County	Distribution	
Genthon		Wpg Grandvital		Dy ex Sun. 15.00 4:00 4/ 14.4

OFFICE	KEY No.	COUNTY		DISTRIBUTION	
Gardenton.........	εe	Provencher....	B. L. & W..... E. & W.	Emerson.......	Dy. tr. 106.
Garland..........	12	Dauphin.......	W. & *S.R*.....	....	Dy. trs. 3, 4.
Garson Quarry.....	8	Selkirk........	Winnipeg.......	Tyndal........	Dy. 10.00, 18.45.
Geyser...........	8	Selkirk........	Winnipeg.......	Arborg....... Icelandic River	Mon. Fri. 14.00. Tue. Sat. 8.00.
Gilbert Plains.....	2	Dauphin.......	W. & *H /Kam*.	....	Dy. trs. 1, 2.
Gimli............	8	Selkirk........	Winnipeg......	....	Dy. tr. 235 C.P.R..
Giroux...........	8a	Provencher....	Ft. F. & W....	....	Dy. tr. 22,
Gladstone.........	7	P. la Prairie....	W. & Y.. W. & *H /Kam*.	....	Dy. trs. 57, 58. Dy. * trs. 1, 2.
Glenboro.........	5	P. la Prairie....	W. & S.......	....	Dy. trs. 55, 56.
Glencairn.........	2	Dauphin.......	W. & *H*. (1)..	....	T. W. T. F. tr. 1.
Glendale..........	3	P. la Prairie....	W. & Y.......	Franklin.......	Tu. Fri. 13.30.
Glendinning.......	6	Souris..........	W. &. N......	Killarney......	Tu. Sat. 8.30.
Glenella..........	2	Dauphin.......	W. &. *H*. (1).	....	Dy. trs. 1, 2.
Glen Elmo........	3b	Marquette.....	W. & Y..... W. & *S.R*	Neepawa......	Rossburn, Tue. Sat. 9.00
Glenforsa.........	3b	Marquette.....	W. & *R*.... W. & Y.....	Neepawa......	M. W. F. tr. 17, C.N.R.
Glenlyon..........	2b	Dauphin.......	W. & *H /Kam*	Gilbert Plains..	Sat. 12.00.
Glenora..........	6	Souris..........	W. & N...... W. & V.......	*Holmfield* Greenway......	Mon. Wed. ...at. tr. 118, C.N.R. Tu. Sat. tr. 117. C.N.R.
Golden Stream.....	2	P. la Prairie....	W. & *H*. (1)...	....	T. T. S. tr. 1.
Gonor............	8	Selkirk........	Winnipeg.......	Lockport......	Mon. Fri. 11.00.
Goodlands.........	6	Souris.........	W. & N...... Deloraine.....	....	Dy. tr. 121 via 139-271. Dy. trs. 139-271-C.P.R.
Goulbourne........	8	Dauphin.......	Winnipeg......	Ashern........	Sat. 9.00.
Grahamdale.......	8	Dauphin.......	Winnipeg......	....	M W. F. tr. 9.
Grand Clariere.....	4	Souris........	W. & V......	....	Dy. tr. 11.
Grande Pointe......	8e	Provencher....	B. L. & W....	....	Dy. trs. 109, 110.
Grand Rapids......	7	Keewatin.....	Winnipeg..... W. & *S.R.P.H*	Selkirk........ Mafeking......	(S) Mon. 7.00. (W) 5th each month.
Grand View........	2c	Dauphin.......	W. & *H.Kam*	....	Dy. trs. 1, 2.
(1) Grandvital.........	8	Provencher.....	Winnipeg......	~~St. Boniface~~....	Dy. ~~13.30~~. *ex Sun. 14.25*
2. Grange...........	5	Macdonald.....	W. & S........	Cypress River..	M. W. F. 14.30.

(1) *Change to St. Vital...* . . .
2. *closed send to Cypress River* {1.1.16 {1.2.16

OFFICE	KEY No.	COUNTY	DISTRIBUTION

OFFICE	KEY No.	COUNTY	DISTRIBUTION		
Grass River........	2	Dauphin.......	W. & *H̶* au.	Tenby........	Fri. 12.00.
Graysville..........	4	Macdonald.....	W. & V........	....	Dy. tr. 11.
Greenland........	8a	Provencher.....	Ft. F. & W....	Ste-Annes des Chenes......	Tu. Fri. 10.15.
Green Ridge.......	8e	Provencher.....	B. L. & W....	Dominion City.	M. W. F. 8.00.
Greenway..........	4	Souris.........	{W. & V...... {W. & N......	.... Holmfield......	Dy. trs. 11, 12. W. S. tr. 118, C.N.R.
Greenwald........	8	Selkirk........	Winnipeg......	Beausejour.....	Fri. 14.00.
Gregg.............	21a	P. la Prairie....	W. & R........	....	Dy. tr. 1.
*Gretna..........	8f	Lisgar.........	G. & W.......	....	Dy. tr. 123.
Griswold..........	1	Brandon..:....	W. & M. J.....	....	Dy. trs. 3, 4, 53-54.
Grosse Isle........	8	Selkirk........	Winnipeg......	....	T. T. S. tr. 9. C.N.R.
Grund............	4	Souris.........	W. & V........	Baldur........	Tu. Fri. 15.45.
Grunthal..........	8a	Provencher.....	Ft. F. & W....	Steinbach......	Mon. Fri. 7.45.
Gunton............	8	Selkirk........	Winnipeg......	....	Dy. trs. 107, 229. C.P.R
Gypsumville.......	8	Dauphin.......	Winnipeg......	....	M. W. F. tr. 9.

H
I
J
K
L
M
N
O
P
Q
R
ST
S
T
U
V
W
Z

OFFICE	KEY No.	COUNTY	DISTRIBUTION		

Office	Key No.	County			Distribution	
Haas..............	8	Selkirk........	Winnipeg......	~~Gimli.~~.....	~~Tue. Fri. 13.00.~~ *m. w. y. T. 23;*	
Hadashville.......	8	Provencher.....	Winnipeg.....	Janow	Fri. 14.00.	
Halbstadt.........	8e	Lisgar........	{B. L. & W.... / E. & W.......	}Emerson......	Fri. 13.00.	
Hallboro..........	12	P. la Prairie...	W. & **S. R.**.......	....	Dy. tr. 3.	
Halicz............	2	Dauphin.......	W. & ~~H.~~ *Kauf*	Ashville.......	Fri. 9.00.	
/ ~~Halstead~~..........	2b	Dauphin.......	W. & ~~H.~~...."..	Gilbert Plains..	Fri. 9.00.	
2 ~~Halton~~............	2c	Dauphin.......	W. & ~~H.~~..."..	Grand View....	Sat. 13.30	
Hamiota..........	10	Marquette.....	Brandon.......	....	Dy. tr. 135, C.P.R.	
Hamrlik..........	8	Dauphin.......	Winnipeg......	Arborg........	Thu. 16.00.	
Harding..........	10	Brandon.......	Brandon......	....	Dy. tr. 215, C.P.R.	
Hargrave.........	1	Brandon.......	W. & M. J.....	....	Dy. trs. 53, 54.	
Harlington........	12b	Dauphin.......	W. & **S. R.**....	Swan River....	Kenville, Tue. Sat. 8.00.	
Harmsworth.......	1d	Brandon.......	*53 18#1* ~~W. & M. J.~~ / W. & V.	~~Virden~~........	*Mon-Wed Fri.* ~~Wed. Sat. 16.00.~~ *TS 59. 60*	
Harperville........	8	Macdonald.....	Winnipeg......	Woodlands.....	Fri. 14.00.	
Harrowby.........	3	Marquette.....	W. & Y.......	....	Dy. tr. 57, 58.	
Harte Station......	21a	P. la Prairie....	W. & Riv......	....	Dy. tr. 3.	
Hartney..........	9	Souris.........	{B. & E....... / W. & V.......	....	Dy. trs. 137, 138. / Dy. trs. 11, 12.	
*Haskett..........	6a	Lisgar........	W. & N.......	Morden.......	M. W. F. tr. 140, G.N.R.	
Hayfield..........	10	Brandon.......	Brandon.......	Hayfield St'n..	Tu. Fri. 13.00.	
3 Hayfield Station....	10	Brandon.......	Brandon.......	....	Dy. tr. 196, G.N.R.	
Hayland..........	8	Dauphin	Winnipeg......	Mulvihill......	Fri. 16.00	
Haywood..........	5	Macdonald.....	W. & S.........	....	Dy. trs. 55. 56.	
Hazel Ridge........	8	Selkirk........	Winnipeg......	....	Dy. tr. 2. C.P.R.	
Headingly........	7	Macdonald.....	{W. & S....... / Winnipeg.....	....	Dy. trs. 55, 56. / Dy. tr. 237. C.P.R.	
Heaslip Station.....	10	Brandon.......	Brandon.......	....	Dy. tr. 196. G.N.R.	
Hecla.............	8	Selkirk........	Winnipeg......	~~Gimli~~.........	Icelandic River, Sat. 8.00	
High Bluff.........	3a	P. la Prairie....	W. & Y. (1)....	....	Dy. trs. 57, 58.	
Hilbre.............	8	Dauphin.......	Winnipeg......	....	M. W. F. tr. 9.	
Hilltop............	3b	Marquette.....	{W. & Y... / W. & **S. R.**.}	Neepawa......	Clan William, Mon. Fri. 17.00.	
Hillview..........	1	Brandon.......	W. & M. J.....	Griswold.......	Tu. Fri. 13.30.	

1 closed via Gilbert Plains 1-9-14
2 closed via Grandview
3 changed to Hayfield 1/9/15

OFFICE	KEY No.	COUNTY	DISTRIBUTION

OFFICE	KEY No.	COUNTY			DISTRIBUTION
Hilton.............	10	Souris.........	Brandon...... W. & V...... Belmont.....	....	Dy. tr. 114, C.N.R. Dy. tr. 11, via 113. Dy. tr. 113, C.N.R.
Hnausa...........	8	Selkirk........	Winnipeg......	~~Gimli~~........	Mon. Fri. 8.00. *Wed: train 235*
Hochfield.........	8a	Provencher.....	Ft. F. & W....	Ste-Anne des Chenes......	Greenland, Tu. Fri. 11.30
Hochstadt.........	8a	Provencher.....	Ft. F. & W....	Steinbach......	Mon. Fri. 7.45.
Hodgson...........	8	Dauphin.......	Winnipeg......	Arborg........	Vidir. Tue. 13.00.
Holland...........	5	Macdonald....	W. & S........	....	Dy. trs. 55, 56.
Hollywood.........	3	Dauphin......	~~W. & Y.~~...... *Portage la Prairie* *Langruth*	~~Westbourne~~....	Fri, 7.00.
Holmfield.........	6	Souris.........	W. & N...... W. & V.......	.... Greenway......	Dy. trs. 121, 122. Tu. Fri. tr. 117, C.N.R.
Homewood........	4	Macdonald.....	W. & V........	....	Dy. trs. 11, 12.
Horndean.........	6	Lisgar.........	W. & N.......	....	Dy. tr. 121.
Hove.............	8	Dauphin.......	Winnipeg......	St. Laurent....	Ideal, Tue. Sat. 11.30.
Howardville.......	8	Selkirk........	Winnipeg......	~~Gimli~~........	Icelandic River Sat. 8.00
Hun's Valley......	3	Dauphin.......	W. & Y.......	Franklin.......	Tue. Fri. 8.00.
Husavick..........	8	Selkirk........	Winnipeg......	Winnipeg Beach	Tu. Sat. 11.15.
Hyde Park........	4	Macdonald....	W. & V........	Roscisle.......	Fri. 12.30.
Hyder...... ...	6	Souris.........	W. & N.......	Ninga.........	Wed. Sat. 8.45.
Hyndman.........	3b	Marquette.....	W. & Y...... W. & S. R...	Neepawa.....	M. W. F. tr. 131.

OFFICE	KEY No.	COUNTY	DISTRIBUTION
Idylwild		Wpg, Ashern	Tue. 8.00

OFFICE	KEY No.	COUNTY.	DISTRIBUTION		
Icelandic River.....	8	Selkirk........	Winnipeg......	~~Gimli~~........	Mon. Fri. ~~8.00~~. *No 235*
Ideal.............	8	Macdonald.....	Winnipeg......	St. Laurent....	Tue. Sat. 11.30.
Indianford........	5	Macdonald.....	W. & S........	Rathwell.......	Tu. Sat. 12.00.
Indian Springs......	4	Macdonald.....	W. & V........	....	Dy. tr. 11.
Ingelow...........	21a	P. la Prairie....	W. & Riv......	....	Dy. trs. 1, 2.
Inkster (sub-office) .	......	Selkirk........	Winnipeg......	....	Dy. 14.00.
Inwood...........	8	Dauphin.......	Winnipeg......	....	M. W. F. tr. 129.
Isabella...........	12	Marquette.....	W. &S. R. (1)	....	M. W. F. tr. 3.
			W. & Y.......	Neepawa......	M. W. F. tr. 131.
Isafold...........	3	Dauphin.......	~~W. & Y.~~ *Portage la Prairie*	Westbourne....	Langruth. Fri. 7.00.
Isle des Chenes.....	8e	Provencher.....	B. L. & W.....	Grande Pointe .	Tu. Fri. 10.45.

OFFICE	KEY No.	COUNTY	DISTRIBUTION

OFFICE	KEY No.	COUNTY	DISTRIBUTION		
Janow............	8	Selkirk........	Winnipeg......	....	M. W. F. tr. 22, G.T.P.
Justice...........	21a	Brandon.......	W. & Riv.....	....	Dy. trs. 1, 2.
			W. & M. J....	Douglas Station	M. W. F. 8.30.

OFFICE	KEY No.	COUNTY	DISTRIBUTION
Kalevala	M.	Winnipeg	McColhill Then 12.30

Office	Key No.	County			Distribution	
Kaleida............	6	Lisgar.........	W. & N.......	Manitou.......	T. T. S. 14.00.	
Karnac............	8	Macdonald.....	Winnipeg......	....	Dy. 8.05.	
Katrine............	12	P. la Prairie...	W. & S. R. (1).		Dy. trs. 3, 4.	
Kawende..........	12	Macdonald.....	W. & S. R. (1).		Dy. trs. 3, 4.	
Keld..............	2a	Dauphin.......	{W. & R. New	Dauphin.......	Fri. 8.00.	
			W. & S. R ..}			
Kelloe.............	3	Marquette.....	W. & Y.......	....	Dy. trs. 57, 58.	
Kelvin.............	1a	Macdonald.....	P. la Prairie...	....	~~Wed. Sat. in 1 Central~~ *Mon. Wed. Fri. 9.00*	
Kelwood..........	12	Dauphin.......	W. & S. R. (1).		Dy. trs. 3, 4.	
Kemnay..........	1	Brandon......	W. & M. J.....		Dy. trs. 53, 54.	
Kenton...........	10	Brandon......	Brandon.......		Dy. tr. 215, C.P.R.	
Kenville..........	12b	Dauphin......	W. & S. R....	Swan River....	T.T.S. tr. 142 C.N.R.	
Keyes.............	3	P. la Prairie....	W. & Y.......	....	..Dy. trs. 57, 58.	
Kildonan West.....	8	Selkirk........	Winnipeg......	....	Dy. 7.00.	
Kilkenny..........	8	Dauphin.......	Winnipeg......	Arborg........	Thu. 7.00.	
*Killarney........	6	Souris.........	W. & N.......	....	Dy. trs. 121, 122.	
King Edward......	8	Macdonald.....	Winnipeg......	....	Dy. El. Car.	
Kingsley..........	4	Lisgar.........	W. & V.......	Somerset.......	Mon. Thur. 14.00.	
Kinosota..........	~~3~~	Dauphin......	*Portage la Prairie Campbell* ~~W. & Y.~~	Westbourne....	~~Fri. 8.00.~~ *M. TH. 1500*	
Kirkella..........	1	Brandon......	W. & M. J.....	....	Dy. trs. 53, 54.	
Kirkfield Park.....	8	Macdonald.....	Winnipeg......	....	Dy. 8.05.	
Kirkness..........	8	Selkirk........	Winnipeg......	East Selkirk....	Tue., Fri., 12.00.	
Kleefeld	8a	Provencher....	Ft. F. & W....	Steinbach......	Mon. Fri. 7.45.	
Klondyke.........	8	Selkirk........	Winnipeg......	Hazel Ridge....	Tue. Fri., 10.00.	
Komarno..........	8	Selkirk........	Winnipeg......	....	Dy. tr. 107. C.P.R.	
Kreuzburg........	8	Selkirk........	Winnipeg......	....	Dy. tr. 107 C.P.R.	
Kronsgart.........	6	Lisgar.........	W. & N.......	Plum Coulee...	M. W. F., tr. 349. G.N. R.	

Closed via Hazelridge 1.4.15
Closed 28.8.1914
Closed 30-11-15

K
L
M
N
O
P
Q
R
St
S
T
U
V
W
Z

OFFICE	KEY No.	COUNTY	DISTRIBUTION
Lettonia			{Winnipeg, Fraser & W Mloleon} Lac du Bonnet Fri 14
Little Maple	Man.	Winnipeg	Inwood. Fri. 13.30
Ledwyn		Winnipeg	Icelandic River Sat 14.00

OFFICE	KEY No.	COUNTY	DISTRIBUTION		
La Broquerie	8a	Provencher			Dy. tr. 22.
Lac du Bonnet	7	Selkirk			Dy. tr. 208, C.P.R.
Ladysmith Station	1a	P. la Prairie	Winnipeg Ft. W. & W.	Molson	M. W.F. tr. 5, C.N.R.
			P. la Prairie		
Ladywood	8	Selkirk	Winnipeg	Beausejour	Fri. 14.00.
Lake Francis	8	Macdonald	Winnipeg	Lake Francis Station	Mon. Fri., 12.45.
Lake Francis St'n	8	Macdonald	Winnipeg		M.W.F. tr. 9. C.N.R.
Lakeland	3	P. la Prairie	W. & Y.	Westbourne	Fri. 7.00.
Langruth	3	Dauphin	W. & Y.	Westbourne	Fri. 7.00.
Langvale	4	Souris	W. & V.	Dunrea	Tu. Sat. 16.30.
Lariviere	6	Lisgar	W. & N		Dy. trs. 121, 122.
La Rochelle	8e	Provencher	B. L. & W	Dufrost	Dy. 19,30.
La Salle	8f	Macdonald	G. & W		Dy. trs. 123, 124.
Lauder	9	Souris	B. & E.		Dy. trs. 137, 138.
Laurier	12	Dauphin	W. & P. A. (1)		Dy. trs. 3, 4.
Lavenham	1a	Macdonald	Pr. la Prairie		Dy. tr. 5, C.N.R.
Lavinia	12	Marquette	W. & A. W. & Y.	Neepawa	M.W.F. tr. 3. M. W.F. tr. 131.
Leary	4	Macdonald	W. & V		Dy. tr. 11.
Leifur	3	Dauphin	W. & Y.	Westbourne	Fri. 7.00.
Lena	6	Souris	W. & N.	Holmfield	Tu. Fri. tr. 117, C.N.R.
Lennard	3c	Marquette	W. & Y.	Russell	Assessippi, Tue., Fri., 13.30.
Lenore	10	Brandon	Brandon		Dy. tr. 215. C.P.R.
*Le Pas	12a	Keewatin	W. & P. A.	Hudson's Bay Junction	T.T.S. tr. 143.
Letellier	8d	Provencher	E. & W		Dy. trs. 7, 8.
Libau	8	Selkirk	Winnipeg	East Selkirk	Sat. 7.00.
Lidford	3	Marquette	W. & Y.	Binscarth	Sat. 11.00.
Lidstone	12	Dauphin	W. & P. A.	Minitonas	W. Sat. 14.15.
Lillesve	8	Dauphin	Winnipeg	Lundar	Otto, Tu. Sat. 13.30.
Lillyfield	8	Selkirk	Winnipeg		T. T. S. 13.00.
Lily Bay	8	Dauphin	Winnipeg	Lundar	Minnewakan, Tue. Sat. 9.00.

L
M
N
O
P
Q
R
ST
S
T
U
V
W
Z

Office	Key No.	County	Distribution
onely Lake		W & M.	Makinak. St Rosedu Lac. Shergrove Set q45

OFFICE	KEY No.	COUNTY	DISTRIBUTION		
Lintrathen........	4	Macdonald.....	W. & V........	Graysville......	Mon. Fri. 11.45.
Loch Monar.......	8c	Macdonald.....	Winnipeg......	Inwood........	Fri. 14.00.
Lockport..........	8	Selkirk........	Winnipeg......	....	Dy. 7.00.
Logoch...........	22	Marquette.....	Riv. & Wain(1)	Oakner........	Sat. 8,30.
Longburn.........	3	Pr. laPrairie....	W. & Y........	Macdonald.....	Tu. Thu. Sat. 11.30.
Loretto....,......	8	Provencher.....	Winnipeg......	....	M.W.F. tr. 22, C. N.R.
Lothair...........	10	Brandon......	Brandon.......	Wheatland.....	Tu. Sat. 10.00.
Louise Bridge (sub Office)............	.....	Provencher.....	Winnipeg......	....	Dy. 13.15.
Lowe Farm........	8	Provencher.....	Winnipeg......		Dy. tr. 15, C.N.R.
Lower Fort Garry...	8	Selkirk........	Winnipeg......		Dy. 7.00.
Lundar...........	8	Dauphin......	Winnipeg......		Mon. Wed. Fri. tr. 9.
Lydiatt...........	8	Selkirk........	Winnipeg......	....	Dy. tr. 2.
Lyleton...........	6	Souris........	W. & N.......	....	Dy. tr. 121 via 139, 271.
			Deloraine.....	....	Dy. tr. 139, 271, C.P.R.

M
N
O
P
Q
R
Sᵀ
S
T
U
V
W
Z

Office	Key No.	County	Distribution
marble Ridge			Winnipeg Arborg Vidir Tue 13.
Marina			Portage la P. Amaranth Sat 8.00

OFFICE	KEY No.	COUNTY	DISTRIBUTION		
McAuley.........	1	Marquette.....	B. & S. (1).....	....	Dy. trs. 59, 60.
McCreary.........	12	Dauphin.......	W. & H. A. (1).	....	Dy. trs. 3, 4.
McConnell........	12	Marquette.....	{W. & S. R. (1) / W. & Y.......	.... / Neepawa......	M. W. F. tr. 3. / M. W. F. tr. 131.
McKenzie.........	6	Lisgar.........	W. & N......	Snowflake......	Tue. Fri. 15.45.
McTavish.........	8f	Provencher.....	G. & W........	....	Dy. trs. 123, 124.
Macdonald........	3	Pr.la Prairie...	W. & Y........	....	Dy. trs. 57, 58.
Macgregor........	1b	Pr.la Prairie...	{W. & M. J.... / Winnipeg.....	....	Dy. trs. 53, 54. / Dy. tr. 101.
Macross..........	8	Dauphin.......	Winnipeg......	Eriksdale......	Pine View Tue. Sat. 11.00.
Madeline.........	3	Marquette.....	W. & Y........	Binscarth......	Mon. 13.00.
Madford..........	1	Brandon......	W. & M.J.....	Douglas St'n...	Mon. Wed. Fri. 8.30.
Mafeking.........	12a	Dauphin.......	S. & P.A	....	Dy. trs. 3, 4.
Magnet...........	12	Dauphin.......	W. & H. (1).	Makinak......	East Bay, Tu. F. 7.00.
Makaroff.........	2	Marquette.....	W. &	....	Dy. tr. 1.-
Makinak..........	12	Dauphin......	W. & P.A. (1).	....	Dy. trs. 3, 4.
Malonton.........	8	Selkirk........	Winnipeg.....	....	Dy. tr. 107. C.P.R.
Manda...........	11	Brandon......	S. & R	Reston.......	Sat. 16.00.
Manigotogan......	8	Selkirk........	Winnipeg.....	....	{Hecla, every 2nd Thu. / 9.00.
Manitou..........	6	Lisgar.........	W. & N......	....	Dy. trs. 121, 122.
Manson..........	1	Marquette.....	B. & S. (1).....	....	Dy. trs. 59, 60.
Marchand........	8a	Provencher....	Ft. F. & W...	....	Dy. tr. 22.
Marco...........	3b	Marquette.....	{W. & Y. / W. & S. R.	Neepawa......	Rossburn..Sat. 14.00.
Margaret.........	4	Souris........	W. & V......	....	Dy. trs. 11, 12.
Mariapolis........	4	Macdonald....	W. & V......	....	Dy. trs. 11, 12.
Markland.........	8	Dauphin.......	Winnipeg......	Inwood........	St. Adelard, Sat. 13.30.
Marney..........	3	Marquette.....	W. & Y.......	Strathclair St'n.	Wed. Sat. 15.15.
Marquette........	3a	Macdonald....	W. & Y. (1).	....	Dy. trs. 57, 58.
Marringhurst......	6	Souris.........	{W. & N..... / W. & V.....	Holmfield.... / Greenway.....	Glenora, Tue. Sat. 9.00.
Mary Hill.........	8	Dauphin.......	Winnipeg......	Lundar........	Mon. Fri. 14.30.

M
N
O
P
Q
R
ST
S
T
U
V
W
Z

Office	Key No.	County	Distribution

OFFICE	KEY No.	COUNTY	DISTRIBUTION		
Maskawata	1	Brandon	W. & M. J.	Griswold	Tu. Fri. 14. 15.
Mather	6	Souris	W. & N.		Dy. trs. 121, 122.
Mayfeld Station	12	P.la Prairie	W. & S.R. (1)		Dy. tr. 3.
Mayne	10	Brandon	Brandon	Wheatland	Sat. 10.00.
Meadow Lea	8	Macdonald	Winnipeg	Warrenton	M. W. F. 12.30.
Meadows	3a	Macdonald	W. & Y. (1)		Dy. trs. 57, 58.
Meadowvale	8	Selkirk	Winnipeg		Tu. Fri. 7.00.
Medora Station	6	Souris	W. & N.		Dy. trs. 121, 122.
Mekiwin	3	P.la Prairie	W. & Y.	Keyes	T. T. S. 12.30.
Melbourne	1	P.la Prairie	W. & M.J.		Tu. Fri. tr. 53.
Meleb	8	Selkirk	Winnipeg		Dy. tr. 107.
*Melita	9	Souris	B. & E.		Dy. trs. 137, 138.
Melrose	8	Selkirk	Winnipeg	East Selkirk	Tue. Fri. 12.00.
Melton	12a	Dauphin	W. & S.R.	Sifton	Sat. 13.00.
Menisino	8e	Provencher	{B. L. & W. / E. & W.}	Emerson	Dy. tr. 106, C.N.R.
Mentieth	9	Brandon	B. & E.		Dy. tr. 137.
Menzie	3b	Marquette	Neepawa		M. W. F. tr. 17, C.N.R.
Merridale	2	Marquette	W. & Alfam	Roblin	Tue. Sat. 13.00.
Methven	5	Brandon	W. & S.		Dy. trs. 55, 56.
Mezieres	5	Macdonald	W. & S.	St. Claude	Sat. 13.00.
Miami	8	Macdonald	Winnipeg		Dy. tr. 15. C.N.R.
Middle Church	8	Selkirk	Winnipeg		Dy. 7.00.
Millbrook	8	Selkirk	Winnipeg		Tu. Fri. 7.00.
Mill Creek	21a	Macdonald	W. & Riv.	Fortier	Fri. 10.30.
Million	12	Dauphin	W. & A. (1)	Makinak	East Bay, Tu. Fr. 14.00.
Millwood	3	Marquette	W. & Y.		Dy. trs. 57, 58.
Miniota	10	Marquette	{Riv. & Wain / Brandon}		Dy. trs. 1, 2. / Dy. tr. 135, C.P.R.
Minitonas	12	Dauphin	W. & S.R.		Dy. trs. 3, 4.
Mink Creek	12a	Dauphin	W. & S.R.	Ethelbert	Sat. 14.00.
*Minnedosa	3	Marquette	W. & Y.		Dy. trs. 57, 58.
Minnewakan	8	Dauphin	Winnipeg	Lundar	Tue. Sat. 9.00.

changed to Medora 1/9/15
) closed via Wheatland.

N
O
P
Q
R
S^T
S
T
U
V
W
Z

Office	Key No.	County		Distribution		
Moose Bay	m	W. *Kane.* R.R. makinak	million		Sat 11.30	
Morweena		Wpg. Arborg – Vidir			Yu. 14.00	
Mountainside	M.	Wpg. Map. whitewater			Lue Thur. Sat 10.00	

OFFICE	KEY No.	COUNTY	DISTRIBUTION			
Minto............	4	Souris........	W. & V.......	....	Dy. trs. 11, 12.	
			Brandon......	....	Dy. tr. 196 G.N.R.	
Moline............	10	Marquette.....	W. & Y......	Rapid City.....	M. W. F. tr. 131.	
			Brandon.....			
Molson...........	7	Selkirk........	Ft. Wm. & W.	....	Dy. trs. 1, 2.	
			Winnipeg.....	....	Dy. tr. 208, C. P. R.	
Monominto........	8a	Provencher.....	Ft. F. & W....	Rosewood......	Tu. Sat. 15.00.	
Moorepark........	1b	Marquette.....	W. & M.J.....	Macgregor....	M.W.F. tr. 219.	
				Douglas Stn..	M. W. F. 8.30.	
Moosehorn........	8	Dauphin.......	Winnipeg.....	....	M. W. F. tr. 9.	
Moose Lake.......	12a	Keewatin.....	W. & P.A......	Hud. Bay Jct..	Le Pas, monthly.	
*Morden..........	6a	Lisgar........	W. & N......	....	Dy. trs. 121, 122.	
Morris............	7	Provencher.....	E. & W........	....	Dy. trs. 7, 8.	
			W. & N......	....	Dy. trs. 121, 122.	
			~~Winnipeg~~....	....	~~Dy. tr. 15.~~	
			G. & W......	....	Dy. trs. 123, 124.	
Morse Place.......	8	Selkirk........	Winnipeg......	Louise Bridge..	M.W.F. 10.45.	
~~Mountain Gap~~.....	2c	Dapuhin.......	W. & ~~H~~ Kaw.	Grand View....	Sat. 13.00.	
Mountain Road....	3	Dauphin.......	W, & Y........	Franklin.......	Tue. Fri. 8.00.	
Mount Royal......	8	Macdonald.....	Winnipeg......	....	T. T. S. 13.00.	
Mowbray..........	6	Lisgar.........	W. & N.....	....	M.W.F. tr. 249, C.P.R.	
			La Riviere...			
Mulvihill..........	8	Dauphin.......	Winnipeg......	....	M.W.F. tr. 9, C.N.R.	
Murchison........	3	Marquette.....	W. & Y........	Franklin.......	Tue. Fri. 8.00.	
Murray Park.......	8	Macdonald.....	Winnipeg......	....	Dy. tr. 55, C.P.R.	
Myrtle...........	8	Lisgar.........	Winnipeg......	....	Dy. tr. 5, C.N.R.	

1 closed via Grandview

N

O

P

Q

R

ST

S

T

U

V

W

Z

Office	Key No.	County	Distribution		

Office	Key No.	County	Distribution ·		
Napinka..........	6	Souris........	W. & N......	....	Dy. tr. 121.
			B. & E.......	....	Dy. tr. 137, 138.
Narol............	8	Selkirk.......	Winnipeg.....	St. Andrews...	Mon. Thu. 10.45.
Neelin............	6	Souris........	W. & N......	Holmfield....	tr. 118, C.N.R.
			W. & V......	Greenway......	T. tr. 117, C.N.R.
*Neepawa.........	3	P. la Prairie....	W. & Y.....	....	Dy. trs. 57, 58.
			W. & P. A.	....	Dy. trs. 3, 4.
Nes.............	8	Selkirk.......	Winnipeg.....	Gimli........	M. Fri. 8.00. *train No 235*
Nesbitt...........	5	Brandon.......	W. & S.......	....	Dy. trs. 55, 56.
Nettly Lake.......	8	Selkirk.......	Winnipeg.....	....	Tu. Th. tr. 235, C.P.R.
Neveton..........	8	Dauphin.......	Winnipeg.....	Inwood........	St. Adelard, Sat. 12.00.
Newdale..........	3	Marquette.....	W. & Y......	....	Dy. trs. 57, 58.
New Sydenham.....	5	Macdonald....	W. & S......	Elm Creek.....	Fri. 13.00.
Ninette...........	4	Souris........	W. & V......	....	Dy. trs. 11, 12.
Ninga............	6	Souris........	W. & N......	....	Dy. trs. 121, 122.
Niverville.........	8e	Provencher....	B. L. & W....	....	Dy. trs. 109, 110.
Norgate..........	12	Dauphin......	W. & P. A. (1).	....	Dy. tr. 3.
Norris Lake.......	8	Selkirk.......	Winnipeg.....	Inwood........	Sat. 11.00.
North Star........	6a	Lisgar........	W. & N......	Morden........	Tu. Fri. 14.00.
North Transcona...	8	Selkirk.......	Winnipeg.....	....	Dy. tr. 2, C.P.R.
Norway House.....	8	Keewatin......	Winnipeg.....	Gimli.....(W)	Icelandic Riv., every second Sat. *Win*
				Selkirk......(S)	2 per week. *Weekly S.*
Norwood Grove....	8	Provencher....	Winnipeg.....	....	Dy. 8.00, 13.30, 18.30.
Notre Dame de Lourdes........	4	Macdonald.....	W. & V.......	....	Dy. tr. 11.

Closed via Elm Creek 1.4.15

N
O
P
Q
R
S[T]
S
T
U
V
W
Z

OFFICE	KEY No.	COUNTY		DISTRIBUTION	
Czerna	to r/ w. r ø A C. R.	Nepawa - Sandy Lake			Mon. Fri. 10.30

OFFICE	KEY No.	COUNTY	DISTRIBUTION		
Oak Bank.........	8	Selkirk........	Winnipeg......	....	Dy. tr. 2, C.P.R.
Oak Bluff..........	8	Macdonald.....	Winnipeg *(index*		M. F. tr. 11, C.N.R.
Oakbrae..........	2a	Dauphin.......	{ W. & *Kam* { W. & S. R.	Dauphin.......	Fork River, Sat. 15.00.
Oakburn..........	3b	Marquette....	{ W. & S. R.. { W. & Y.....	Neepawa......	M. W. F. tr. 17, C.N.R.
Oak Hammock.....	8	Selkirk........	Winnipeg......	Low. Ft. Garry.	Fri. 10.30.
Oak Lake.........	1	Brandon.......	{ W. & M. J.... { { B. & S........	....	{ Dy. trs. 53, 54. { Dy.* trs. 3, 4. Dy. trs. 59, 60.
Oakland..........	1a	P. la Prairie....	P. la Prairie....		T. T. S. 13.00.
Oakner..........	21a	Marquette....	Riv. & Wain (1)	....	Dy. tr. 2.
Oaknook..........	2b	Dauphin.......	W. & *Kam*	Gilbert Plains..	Tu. F. 13,15.
Oak Point........	8	Macdonald....	Winnipeg......	....	M.W.F. tr. 9, C.N.R.
Oak River........	10	Marquette.....	Brandon........		Dy. tr. 135, C.P.R.
Oakview..........	8	Dauphin.......	Winnipeg......	Mulvihill.....	{ Dog Creek. { Tue. 9.00, Fri. 16.00.
Oatfield..........	8	Dauphin.......	Winnipeg......	Mulvihill......	Tue. 9.00, Fri. 16.00.
Oberon..........	1b	P. la Prairie....	W. & M. J....	Macgregor....	M.W.F. tr. 219, C.P.R.
Ochre River.......	12	Dauphin.......	W. & P. A. (1).. *Kam*	....	Dy. tr.s.
Ogilvie Station.....	2	P. la Prairie....	W. & *Kam*..	....	Dy. tr. 1.
Okno.............	8	Selkirk........	Winnipeg......	Arborg........	Vidir, Fri. 8.00.
Olha.............	3b	Marquette....	W. & Y { W. & B. R...	Neepawa.......	Oakburn Wed. Sat. 12.00.
Olive.............	5	Macdonald.....	W. & S........	Treherne.......	Tu. Sat. 13.00.
Orrwold..........	12	Marquette....	{ W. & S. R.... { W & Y....... Neepawa.....		Decker, T.T.S. 10.00.
Osborne Station....	8f	Macdonald.....	G. & W........		Dy. trs. 123, 124.
Oswald..........	8	Macdonald....	Winnipeg......	Warrenton.....	M.W.F. 12.30.
Otterburne........	8e	Provencher.....	B. L. & W......		Dy. trs. 109, 110.
Otto.............	8	Dauphin.......	Winnipeg......	Lundar........	Mon. Fri. 14.45........
Owoju............	1	Brandon.......	W. & M. J.....	Griswold.......	Tue. Fri. 16.30.

Changed to Osborne 1/9/15

O
P
Q
R
ST
S
T
U
V
W
Z

OFFICE	KEY No.	COUNTY	DISTRIBUTION

OFFICE	KEY No.	COUNTY	DISTRIBUTION		
.cific Junction....	8	Macdonald.....	Winnipeg......	....	Dy. tr. 3, G.T.P.
.rkdale..........	8	Selkirk........	Winnipeg......	....	Dy. 7.00.
.bble Beach......	8	Dauphin.......	Winnipeg.....	Mulvihill.......	Tue. 9.00 Fri. 16.00.
.guis.............	8b	Selkirk........	Winnipeg.......	..Selkirk	Tue. Fri. 8.00.
.lican Rapids.....	12a	Dauphin........ S.G. & P. A.....	{Barrows.....	Monthly 9th each month (s)	
			{Mafeking.....	Fortnightly every 2nd Friday (w)	
.ndennis..........	10	Brandon.......	Brandon.......	....	Dy. tr. 215 C.P.R.
.trel.............	1c	P. laPrairie....	{Carberry......	....	M. W. F. tr. 115. C.N.R.
			{Neepawa.....	....	T.T.S. tr. 116, C.N.R.
.ttapiece.........	10	Marquette.....	Brandon.......	....	Dy. tr. 135. C.P.R.
.erson............	9	Souris.........	B. & E........	....	Dy. trs. 137, 138.
.geon Bluff.......	8	Selkirk........	Winnipeg.....	Low. Ft. Garry	Mon. Wed. Fri. 12.00.
.geon Lake.......	7	Macdonald.....	{W. & S...... {Winnipeg....	Headingly.....	Dy. 10.30.
.ilot Mound.......	6	Lisgar.........	W. & N........	....	Dy. trs. 121, 122.
.inawa............	7	Selkirk........	{Ft. W. & W... {Winnipeg.....	Molson........	Lac du Bonnet....... M. W. F. 10.00.
.ne Creek Stn.....	1b	P. la Prairie...	W. & M. J.....	Macgregor.....	M. W. F. tr. 219.
.ine Ridge........	8	Selkirk........	Winnipeg......	Oak Bank......	Fri. 9.30.
.ine River Station..	12	Dauphin.......	W. & S. R.	....	Dy. tr. 3.
.ne View.........	8	Dauphin.......	Winnipeg.....	Eriksdale.......	Mon. Fri. 15.00.
.ney.............	8e	Provencher.....	{E. & W...... {B. L. & W....	{Emerson.......	Dy. tr. 106, C.N.R.
.pestone..........	11	Brandon.......	S. & R........	....	Dy. trs. 55, 56.
.easant Home.....	8	Selkirk........	Winnipeg.....	Komarno......	Mon. Fri. 14.30.
.umas............	2	Dauphin.......	W. & K. (1)..	....	Dy. trs. 1, 2.
.um Coulee.......	6	Lisgar.........	W. & N.......	....	Dy. trs. 121, 122.
.ympton..........	8	Selkirk........	Winnipeg.....	....	Tu. Fri. 7.00.
.meroy..........	8	Macdonald.....	Winnipeg......	Roland........	Sat. 12.09.
.pe.............	21a	Marquette.....	Riv. & Wain.(1)	....	Dy. tr. 2.......
.plarfield.........	8	Dauphin.......	Winnipeg.....	Arborg........	Broad Valley. Sat. 9.00.
.plar Park........	8	Selkirk........	Winnipeg.....	East Selkirk....	Sat. 7.30.
.plar Point.......	3a	Macdonald.....	W. & Y. (1)....	....	Dy. trs. 57, 58.

hanfeld to Pine River 1/9/15

OFFICE	KEY No.	COUNTY	DISTRIBUTION

OFFICE	KEY No.	COUNTY.	DISTRIBUTION		
Portage la Prairie..	1	P. la Prairie....	W. & M. J....	....	Dy. *trs. 3, 4, 61, 62.
					Dy. trs. 53, 54.
			W. & Y....	....	Dy. trs. 57, 58.
			W. & S. A....	....	Dy. trs. 3, 4.
			W. & H. Rams....	....	Dy. *trs. 1, 2.
			Winnipeg....	....	Dy. tr. 101, C.P.R.
					Dy. *tr. 1, C.P.R.
			W. & Riv....	....	Dy. trs. 1, 2.
Prairie Grove......	8	Selkirk........	Winnipeg....	....	M. F. tr. 22, C.N.R.
Pratt.............	1a	Macdonald.....	P. la Prairie....	....	M.W.F. tr. 5, C.N.R.
Purple Ridge.......	2	Dauphin.......	W. & H. (1)....	Glenella......	Sat. 12.30.
Purves...........	6	Lisgar........	W. & N....	....	M.W.F. tr. 121via 249
			Lariviere....	....	M.W.F. tr. 249, C.P.R.

OFFICE	KEY No.	COUNTY	DISTRIBUTION

OFFICE	KEY No.	COUNTY	DISTRIBUTION		
ns Valley......	8	Selkirk........	Winnipeg........	....	Tu. Fri. 7.00.

Q
R
S^T
S
T
U
V
W
Z

OFFICE	KEY No.	COUNTY	DISTRIBUTION		
Regent		{ W. n Brandon }	Boisevain		

Office	Key No.	County	Distribution		
Rabbit Point.......	8	Dauphin.......	Winnipeg......	Lundar........	Tue. Sat. 9.00.
Radway...........	8	Dauphin.......	Winnipeg......	Clarkleigh.....	Mon. Fri. 14.15.
Ranchvale........	3b	Marquette....	{W. & Y....}{W. & S. R..}	Neepawa......	Rossburn, Tue. Sat. 8.30
Rapid City........	10	Marquette....	{Brandon.....}{W. & Y......}	....	Dy. tr. 135 C.P.R. Dy. trs. 57, 58, via 256 C.P.R.
Rateau...........	8	Selkirk........	Winnipeg.....	....	M.W.F. tr. 22, G.T.P.
Rathwell..........	5	Macdonald.....	W. & S........	....	Dy. trs. 55, 56.
Reaburn..........	3a	Macdonald.....	W. & Y. (1)....	....	Dy. trs. 57, 58.
Reinland..........	8f	Lisgar.........	G. & W.......	Gretna........	Tu. Fri. 13.00.
Rembrandt.......	8	Selkirk........	Winnipeg.....	....	Dy. tr. 107 C.P.R.
Rennie...........	5	Selkirk........	Ft. Wm. & W..	....	Dy. trs. 1, 2.
Reston...........	11	Brandon.......	{S. & R.......}{R. & W......}	....	Dy. trs. 55, 56. Dy. tr. 246.
Reykjavik........	8	Dauphin.......	Winnipeg......	Mulvihill......	The Narrows, Sat. 14.00.
Richer............	8a	Provencher....	Ft. F & W.....	Ste. Anne des Chenes......	Mon. Fri. 13.15.
Richland..........	8	Selkirk........	Winnipeg.....	....	Tu. Fri. 7.00.
Ridgely...........	8	Selkirk........	Winnipeg......	Low Ft. Garry.	Mon. Wed. Fri. 12.00.
Ridgeville.........	8e	Provencher....	{E. & W.....}{B. L. & W ..}	Emerson.......	Dy. tr. 106, C.N.R.
Ridgeway.........	12	Macdonald.....	W. & S. R (1).	....	W. F. tr. 3.
Riding Mountain...	12	Dauphin.......	W. & S. R (1).	....	Dy. trs. 3, 4.
Riel..............	8	Provencher....	Winnipeg......	St. Boniface...	T.T.S. 10.00.
Ritchot...........	8	Provencher....	Winnipeg......	St. Boniface....	T.T.S. 10.00.
Rivers...........	21a	Brandon.....	{Wpg. & Riv..}{Riv. & Wain..}	....	Dy. *trs. 1, 2.
Roblin............	2	Marquette.....	W. & Maus	....	Dy. trs. 1, 2.
Roden............	1	Brandon.......	W. & M. J.....	Griswold.......	Tu. Fri. 13.30.
Roland...........	8	Macdonald....	Winnipeg.....	....	Dy. tr. 15, C.N.R.
Rolling River.......	3	Marquette.....	W. & Y.......	Basswood......	Mon. Thu. 14.30.
Rosa.............	8e	Provencher....	{E. & W.....}{B. L. & W...}	Emerson.......	Stuartburn, Fri. 13.00.
Rosebank.........	8	Macdonald.....	Winnipeg......	....	Dy. tr. 15, C.N.R.
Roseisle..........	4	Macdonald.....	W. & V........	....	Dy. trs. 11, 12.

R
ST
S
T
U
V
W
Z

OFFICE	KEY No.	COUNTY	DISTRIBUTION	
Rosenburg		Wpg–Arborg–Vidir–Okno		Sat. 16.³⁰

OFFICE	KEY No.	COUNTY.	DISTRIBUTION		
osenfeld.........	6	Lisgar........	W. & N......	....	Dy. trs. 121, 122.
			G. & W......	....	Dy. trs. 123, 124.
osenort..........	8f	Provencher....	G. & W.......	McTavish......	M. W. F. 15.00.
osewood.........	8a	Provencher....	Ft. F. & W ... *f. 7.f. f.'fu)*		M. W. F. tr. 22.
ossburn..........	3b	Marquette....	W. & Y......	Russell........	T.T.S. tr. 18, C.N.R.
			W. & Y..		M.W.F. tr. 17, C.N.
			W. & S. R...	Neepawa......	R.
ossendale........	1a	P.la Prairie....	P. la Prairie....	....	Dy. tr. 5. C.N.R.
osser.............	3a	Macdonald.....	W. & Y. (1)....	....	Dy. trs. 57, 58.
ounthwaite......	10	Brandon.....	W. & V......	....	Dy. tr. 11, via 45.
			Belmont......		Dy. tr. 113, C.N.R.
			Brandon.		Dy. tr. 114, C.N.R.
outledge..........	1	Brandon.......	W. & M. J	....	T. T. S. tr. 53.
ussell............	3c	Marquette....	W. & Y......	....	Dy. tr. 57, via 253.
			Binscarth		Dy. tr. 253, C.P.R.
			W. & S. K....	Neepawa......	M. W. F. tr. 17, C.N.R.
uth.............	9	Souris........	B. & E.......	Melita........	*MWF. T137 via 254*
				Lauder	*M W F. T12 54*
utherford........	1b	P.la Prairie....	W. & M.J..	Macgregor.....	Edrans, Fri. 11.30.
			Winnipeg.....	*an argutl*	
yanton..........	3	Dauphin.......	W. & Y.......	Westbourne....	Leifur, Sat. 15.00.

S^T

S

T

U

V

W

Z

Office	Key No.	County	Distribution		
St Lionel		..	Wipeg	Arborg	Fisherton / sat 1800

OFFICE	KEY No.	COUNTY	DISTRIBUTION		
St. Adelard........	8	Dauphin......	Winnipeg......	Inwood........	~~Fri. 8.00.~~ *Sat 7.45*
St. Adolphe........	8	Provencher....	Winnipeg......	....	M.W.F. tr. 15, C.N.R.
Ste. Agathe........	8	Provencher....	Winnipeg......	....	Dy. tr. 15, C.N.R.
St. Alphonse.......	4	Macdonald.....	W. & V.......	Mariapolis.....	M.W.F.S. 15.00.
St. Ambroise........	3a	Macdonald....	W.& Y. (1)....	Poplar Point...	Tu. Fri. 10.30.
Ste. Amelie........	-12	Dauphin......	W. & *Kaul* (1)	Makinak.......	T.T.S. 7.30.
St. Andrews........	8	Selkirk........	Winnipeg......	....	Dy. 7.00.
Ste.Anne des Chenes	8a	Provencher....	Ft. F. & W....	....	Dy. trs. 21, 22.
St. Boniface.......	8	Provencher....	Winnipeg.......	....	Dy. ~~8.00~~, ~~15.30~~, ~~17.00~~.
St. Charles........	8	Macdonald....	Winnipeg......	....	Dy. 7.30.
St. Claude........	5	Macdonald....	W. & S........	....	Dy. trs. 55, 56.
St. Daniel........	5a	Macdonald....	{W. & V...... / W. & S......}	Carman.......	Fri. 13.00.
Ste. Elizabeth.....	7	Provencher....	{W. & N...... / G. & W...... / E. & W...... / Winnipeg....}	Morris........	M. W. F. 12.00.
St. Eustache.......	12	Macdonald....	W. & *Kaul* (1)	Elie...........	Dy. 11.30.
St. Francois Xavier.	7	Macdonald....	{W. & S...... / Winnipeg....}	Headingly.....	Dy. 10.30.
St. George........	7	Selkirk........	{Ft. W. & W... / Winnipeg. ....}	Molson....... /	Lac du Bonnet, ~~Tu.~~ *Fri.* 8.00.
St. James.........	8	Macdonald....	Winnipeg.......	....	Dy. 7.30.
St. Jean Baptiste...	8d	Provencher....	E. & W........	....	Dy. trs. 7, 8.
St. Joseph........	8d	Provencher....	E. & W.......	Letellier.......	M. W. Sat. 9.00.
St. Laurent........	8	Macdonald....	Winnipeg......	....	M. W. F. tr. 9, C.N.R.
St. Labre..........	8a	Provencher....	F. F. & W.....	Woodridge.....	Tue. Fri. 12.30.
St. Lazare.........	22	Marquette....	{Riv. & Wain... / *Woyerk*}	.... / *FOXWARREN*	Dy. *tr. 2. / *Mn. Thu. 10.30*
St. Leon..........	4	Macdonald....	W. & V........	Somerset.......	M. W. F. S. 13.30.
St. Louis Guilbert...	8	Selkirk........	Winnipeg......	....	Dy. tr. 235, C.P.R.
St. Malo..........	8e	Provencher....	B. L. & W.....	Dufrost........	Dy. 18.30.
St. Marks.........	3a	Macdonald.....	W. & Y. (1)....	Poplar Point...	Tu. Fri. 10.00.
St. Martin's Station	8	Dauphin......	Winnipeg....	....	M. W. F. tr. 9.
St. Norbert........	8	Provencher....	Winnipeg......	....	Dy. tr. 15, C.N.R.
St. Ouens.........	8	Selkirk........	Winnipeg......	....	Dy. tr. 112, C.P.R.

59103—5

ST

S

T

U

V

W

Z

Office	Key No.	County	Distribution
Total (Carlrwlil)	*M.*	*Humphreys*	*Dfg 13.30*

Office	Key No.	County			Distribution
St. Pie............	8d	Provencher.....	E. & W........	Letellier.......	Wed. Sat. 11.00.
St. Pierre Jolys.....	8e	Provencher.....	B. L. & W.....	....	Dy. tr. 110.
St. Raymond.......	8a	Provencher.....	Ft. F. & W....	Ste. Anne des Chenes......	Tu. Sat. 10.30.
Ste. Rose du Lac...	12	Dauphin.......	W. & P.~~A.~~ *Kaus* (1).	Makinak.......	T. T. S. 7.30.
St. Vital..........	8	Provencher.....	Winnipeg.....	....	M. T. T. S. 10.30.
Saltel.............	8a	Provencher.....	Ft. F. & W....	Ste. Anne des Chenes......	Sat. 12.30.
Sandilands........	8a	Provencher.....	~~Ft. F. & W~~	~~H.~~	~~Dy. tr. 22~~
Sandridge.........	8	Dauphin.......	Winnipeg......	Inwood........	Sat. 7.00.
Sandy Bay........	3	Dauphin.......	~~W. & Y~~	~~Westbourne~~....	~~Fri. 7.00.~~
Sandy Lake.......	3b	Dauphin.......	{ W. & Y.... / W. & S. R... }	Neepawa......	M. W. F. tr. 17, C.N.R.
Sanford...........	4	Macdonald.....	W. & V. (1)....	....	Dy. trs. 11, 12.
Sarto.............	8a	Provencher.....	Ft. F. & W....	Steinbach......	Grunthal, Fri. 14.00.
Scandinavia.......	3b	Marquette.....	{ W. & Y.... / W. & S. R.. }	Neepawa......	Clan William, Mon. Fri. 17.00.
Scanterbury.......	8	Selkirk........	Winnipeg......	East Selkirk.....	Sat. 7.30.
Scarth............	4	Brandon......	~~W. & V Br. R.~~	....	{ M. W. F. tr. 11 / T. T. S. tr. 12. }
Sclater...........	12	Dauphin.......	W. & S. R....		Dy. tr. 3.
Scotch Bay........	8	Dauphin.......	Winnipeg......	~~Lundar~~.......	~~Minnewakan, Tue. Sat. 9.00.~~
Scotland Farm.....	8	Dauphin.......	Winnipeg......	Arborg........	Thu. 16.00.
Seamo............	8	Dauphin.......	Winnipeg......	Clarkleigh.....	Mon. Fri. 14.15.
Seeburn...........	3	Marquette.....	W. & Y.......	Binscarth......	Sat. 11.00.
Seech.............	3b	Marquette.....	{ W. & Y.... / W. & S. R.. }	Neepawa.... Olha, Sat. 12.00.	
*Selkirk...........	8b	Selkirk........	Winnipeg......	....	{ Dy. tr. 208, C.P.R. / Dy. 14.00. / Dy. tr. 235, C.P.R. }
Senkiw...........	8e	Provencher....	{ E. & W...... / B. L. & W... }	Emerson.......	Stuartburn, Fri. 13.00.
Shadeland.........	6	Lisgar.........	W. & N.......	Darlingford....	M. W. F. 8.00.
Shanawan..........	8f	Macdonald....	G. & W.......	....	Dy. trs. 123, 124.
Shellmouth........	3c	Marquette.....	W. & Y.......	Russell........	M. W. F. tr. 17. C.N.R.

S
T
U
V
W
Z

Office	Key No	County	Distribution			
Skylake			Winnipeg	Rembrandt	Th. 13.	
Stewart Lake			Winnipeg	Camper	Sat 13.	
Shergrove	m		W + Kam Pca	Makinak	St Rose du Lac	Tue 1330
Shortdale			W + Kam.		Ex mon 4⸱1	
Sirko			{E+W}{BF. W}	Emerson	Sundown	Fri 10.30
Spearhill			Winnipeg	Moosehorn	Tue Sat 1100	
Step Rock			Wpeg	Grahamdale	Tues sat 90	

OFFICE	KEY No.	COUNTY	DISTRIBUTION		
Sheppardville......	6b	Souris.........	{W. & N.....} {Brandon.....}	Boissevain.....	Tu. Fri. 9.00.
/ Shiperlay.........	5	Macdonald....	W. & S. (1)....	Starbuck.......	Fri. 11.00.
Shoal Lake........	3	Marquette....	W. & Y........	....	Dy. trs. 57, 58.
Sidney............	1	P. la Prairie....	W. & M. J....	....	Dy. trs. 53, 54.
Sifton............	12	Dauphin......	W. & S. R..	....	Dy. tr. 3.
Siglunes..........	8	Dauphin......	Winnipeg.....	Mulvihill......	Tue. 9.00, Fri. 16.00.
Silver Bay........	8	Dauphin......	Winnipeg.....	Ashern........	Sat. 9.00.
Silverton Station....	3c	Marquette....	{W. & Y....} {W. & S. R..} {W. & Y.....}	Russell........ Neepawa......	T. T. S. tr. 18, C.N.R. M. W. F. tr. 17, C.N.R.
Sinclair Station.....	11	Brandon.......	S. & R........	....	Dy. trs. 55, 56.
Skalholt..........	5	P. la Prairie....	W. & S........	Glenboro......	Fri. 13.30.
Smith Hill........	6	Souris.........	W. & N	Holmfield	Tue. Fri. tr. 117C.N.R.
Snow Flake........	6	Lisgar.........	{W. & N......} {Lariviere......}	....	M. W. F. tr. 121, via 249 M.W.F. tr. 249, C.P.R.
Solsgirth..........	3	Marquette....	W. & Y........	....	Dy. trs. 57, 58.
Somerset..........	4	Macdonald.....	W. & V........	....	Dy. trs. 11, 12.
*Souris...........	5	Brandon......	{W. & S......} {S. & R......} {B. & E......}	....	Dy. tr. 55. Dy. tr. 56. Dy. trs. 137, 138.
Sourisford........	6	Souris.........	W. & N.......	Coulter........	M. F. 14.00.
South Junction.....	8a	Provencher....	{Ft. F. & W...} {B. L. & W...} {E. & W......}	Emerson.......	Dy. trs. 21, 22. T. T. S. tr. 106, C.N.R.
Sperling..........	4	Provencher....	W. & V. (1)....	....	Dy. trs. 11, 12.
*Sprague..........	8a	Provencher....	Ft. F. & W....	....	Dy. trs. 21, 22.
Springfield........	8	Selkirk........	Winnipeg......	....	Dy. tr. 2, C.P.R.
Springhurst........	3	P. la Prairie....	W. & Y........	Franklin.......	Tue. Fri. 8.00.
Springstein........	8	Macdonald.....	Winnipeg......	....	Dy. tr. 55, C.P.R.
Spruce Creek......	2a	Dauphin.......	{W. & Kau} {W. & S. R.}	Dauphin.......	Fri. 8.00.
Spurgrave..........	8a	Provencher....	Ft. F. & W. Ft. F. & W	ells Wd Ft Jr 22 Dy. tr. 22.	
Starbuck..........	5	Macdonald.....	W. & S. (1)....	....	Dy. trs. 55, 56.
Steinbach..........	8a	Provencher....	Ft. F. & W....	....	Dy. tr. 22.
Stephenfield........	4	Macdonald.....	W. & V........	....	Dy. tr. 11.

1 Closed via Starbuck 1.4.15
2 " " Woodridge 1.8.15.

T
U
V
W
Z

OFFICE	KEY No.	COUNTY	DISTRIBUTION
Sloan			Winnipeg Arborg Violet Tue 13

OFFICE	KEY No.	COUNTY	DISTRIBUTION			
Stockton Station...	5	P. la Prairie....	W. & S........	....		Dy. trs. 55, 56.
Stonewall.........	8c	Selkirk........	Winnipeg......	....		Dy. trs. 107, 229, C.P.R.
Stony Hill........	8	Dauphin.......	Winnipeg......	Lundar........		Mon. Fri. 14.45.
Stony Mountain....	8	Selkirk........	Winnipeg......	....		Dy. trs. 107, 229, C.P.R.
Strathclair Station	3	Marquette.....	W. & Y........			Dy. trs. 57, 58.
·Strathewen........	8c	Selkirk........	Winnipeg......	Stonewall.....		Thur. 7.30.
Stuartburn........	8e	Provencher.....	{E. & W...... {B. L. & W...}	Emerson.......		T. T. S. tr. 106, C.N.R.
Sturgeon Creek.....	8	Macdonald....	Winnipeg......	....		Dy. 8.05.
Sundown..........	8e	Provencher.....	{E. & W...... {B. L. & W...}	Emerson.......		T.T.S. tr. 106, C.N.R.
Sunville..........	2	Dauphin.......	W. & H. (1)....	Glenella.......		Fri. 14.00.
Swan Lake........	4	Macdonald....	W. & V........	....		Dy. trs. 11, 12.
Swan River.......	12b	Dauphin.......	W. & S. R....	....		Dy. trs. 3, 4.

1 Changed to Stockton 1/9/15
2 " " Strathclair 1/9/15

T
U
V
W
Z

Office	Key No	County	Distribution		
The Halfway	m.	Wpg., Arborg - Vidir			Tue. 13.00
Tipperary	n.	Wpg, Eriksdale, Vannes			Fri. 18.00
Tuxedo	n.	Wpg			D. ? 121
Trenham	m.	H.T. & Wpg. Steinbach			Fri. 18.00

OFFICE	KEY No.	COUNTY	DISTRIBUTION		
'enby............	2	Dauphin......	W. & *Karru*............		Dy. trs. 1, 2.
'erence............	9a	Brandon......	B. & R........	....	Dy. tr. 6, C.N.R.
'eulon...........	8	Selkirk........	Winnipeg......	....	Dy. tr. 107, C.P.R.
'halberg..........	8	Provencher....	Winnipeg......	Beausejour.....	Fri. 14.00.
The Landing......	3	P. la Prairie....	W. & Y........	Westbourne....	Dy. 11.30.
The Narrows......	8	Dauphin.......	Winnipeg......	Mulvihill.......	Tue. 9.00, Fri. 16.00.
Thornhill.........	6	Lisgar..........	W. & N........	....	Dy. trs. 121, 122.
Thunder Hill......	12b	Dauphin.......	W. & *S. R.*...	Swan River....	Kenville, M. F. 16.00.
Tilston...........	11	Souris........	*B & E.* S. & R. *B & E*	Sinclair St'n...	*Metric 254* *13-8-5.00.* *Wood 1400* *The tr 137 via 254*
Tolstoi...........	8e	Provencher....	{ E. & W...... } { B. L. & W... }	Emerson.......	T.T.S. tr. 106, C.N.R.
Totonka...........	10	Marquette....	Brandon.......	Oak River.....	Tue. Fri. 11.00.
Toutes Aides......	12	Dauphin.......	W. & *Kau.* L A (1).	Makinak.......	Magnet, Tu. 14.00.
Transcona........	8	Selkirk........	Winnipeg......	....	Dy. 9.00.
Tranter...........	8	Dauphin.......	Winnipeg......	Mulvihill......	Tue. 9.00, Fri. 16.00.
Treesbank........	5	P. la Prairie....	W. & S........	....	Dy. trs. 55, 56.
Treherne..........	5	Macdonald....	W. & S........	....	Dy. trs. 55, 56.
Tumbell..........	2	Marquette....	W. & *H Kau*	Roblin.........	Fri. 10.00.
Turtle River......	12	Dauphin.......	W. & *Kau.* L A (1).	Makinak.......	Tu. Fri. 7.00. *m. W. 7. to 59*
Two Creeks.......	10	Marquette.....	{ *B & B # E* Riv. & Wain. Brandon...... }	Miniota.......	Tue. Fri. 9.00.
Tyndall..........	8	Selkirk........	Winnipeg......	....	Dy. tr. 112, C.P.R.

T
U
V
W
Z

Office	Key No	County	Distribution		

OFFICE	KEY No.	COUNTY			DISTRIBUTION	
Ukraina...........	12	Dauphin.......	W. & S. R......	*Grand View*		Dy. tr. 3.
Umatilla..........	2b	Dauphin.......	W. & H. Saw. Gilbert Plains..	~~Fri. 9.00.~~ *Dy. 9³⁰*		
Underhill.........	4	Souris.........	W. & V........	....		Dy. trs. 11, 12.
Union Point.......	8	Provencher.....	Winnipeg......	....		M.W.F. tr. 15, C.N.R.
Uno..............	21a	Marquette.....	Riv. & Wain (1)	....		Dy. tr. 2.

Closed via Grand View 1/9/15

U
V
W
Z

OFFICE	KEY No.	COUNTY	DISTRIBUTION
alpoy			w. ~~Kauy~~. mabinaka St Rose du Lac Sat 1 40
⅄			

OFFICE	KEY No.	COUNTY	DISTRIBUTION		
Valley River	12	Dauphin	W. & S. R.		Dy. tr. 3.
Valley Stream	3b	P. la Prairie	{W. & Y.. {W. & S. R.	Neepawa	Tue. Fri. tr. 4.
Vannes	8	Dauphin	Winnipeg	Eriksdale	Mon. Fri. 15.00.
Vassar	8a	Provencher	E. F. & W.		Dy. trs 21, 22.
Velma	6	Lisgar	W. & N	Snow Flake	M. W. Sat. 15.45.
Venlaw	2b	Dauphin	W. & E.	Gilbert Plains	Tu. F. 13.15.
Vestfold	8	Dauphin	Winnipeg	Clarkleigh	Fri. 14.15.
Vidir	8	Selkirk	Winnipeg	Arborg	Mon. Fri. 13.00.
Vincelette	8	Selkirk	Winnipeg	Lower F. Garry	Fri. 11.45.
Viola Dale	12	Marquette	{W. & S. R.(1) {W. & Y	Neepawa	McConnell, M.W.F 19.00
*Virden	1	Brandon	{W.& M. J {W. & V {B. & S		Dy. trs. 53, 54. Dy.* trs. 3, 4. Dy. tr. 11. Dy. trs. 59, 60.
Vista	3b	P. la Prairie	{W. & S. R. {W. & Y	Neepawa	M. W. F. tr. 17, C.N.R.
Vita	8e	Provencher	{B. L. & W {E. & W	Emerson	T.T.S. tr. 106, C.N.R.
Vivian Station	8	Selkirk	Winnipeg		M.W.F. tr. 22, T.T.S. tr. 21.
Volga	12	Dauphin	{W. & S. R. {W. & E.	Dauphin	Winnipegosis, Fri. 13.00.

1 Closed via Snowflake 1-12-14

V
W
Z

OFFICE	No.	COUNTY	DISTRIBUTION		
Dacouta		W peg	Mulvihill	Frantn Sat 7.⁵⁰	
Litimouth Lake		St. Philips	Vassar	Sat. 13.30	
Willen		Br & Sask.		M.W. Jn. Jns.59,	

OFFICE z	KEY No.	COUNTY	DISTRIBUTION		
Wakopa	6	Souris	W. & N.	Holmfield	Tu. F. tr. 117, C.N.R.
Waldersee	2	Dauphin	W. & H. (1).	Glenella	Tue. Fri. 13.00.
Walkerburn	2	Dauphin	W. & H./Taue	Togo	Fri. 13.00.
Walkleyburg	8	Selkirk	Winnipeg	East Selkirk	Sat. 18.40.
Wampum	8e	Provencher	E. & W., B. L. & W.	Emerson	Dy. tr. 106.
1 Wapaha	6b	Souris	W. & N., Brandon	Boissevain	Sat. 8.30.
Warrenton	8	MacDonald	Winnipeg		M. W. F. tr. 9.
Waskada	6	Souris	W. & N., Deloraine		Dy. tr. 121 via 139, 271. Dy. tr. 139, 271, C.P.R.
Wassewa	6b	Souris	W. & N., Brandon	Boissevain	Fri. 16.00.
Wattsview	3	Marquette	W. & Y.	Birtle	Tu. Fri. 8.00.
Wavy Bank	8c	Selkirk	Winnipeg	Stonewall	Mon. Th. 13.15.
Wawanesa	10	Brandon	W. & V., Belmont tr., Brandon Belmont Brandon		Dy. tr. 11 via 113. Dy. tr. 113, C.N.R. Dy. tr. 114, C.N.R.
Wellwood	1b	P. la Prairie	W. & M. J., Winnipeg	Macgregor	M.W.F. tr. 219, C.P.R.
Westbourne	3	P. la Prairie	W. & Y.		Dy. trs. 57, 58.
West Hall	4	Souris	W. & V.	Underhill	Tue. Fri. 11.00.
West Winnipeg	7	Macdonald	W. & S., Winnipeg	Headingly	Dy. 11.00.
Wheatland	10	Brandon	Brandon		Dy. tr. 215, C.P.R.
Whitemouth	7	Selkirk	Ft. W. & W.		Dy. trs. 1, 2.
Whitewater	6	Souris	W. & N.		Dy. trs. 121, 122.
Whytewold	8	Selkirk	Winnipeg		Dy. tr. 235, C.P.R.
Wild Oak	3	Dauphin	W. & Y. Portage La Prairie Longmuth	Westbourne	Fri. 7.00.
1 Wilford	2b	Dauphin	W. & H./Taue	Gilbert Plains	Sat. 12.30.
Willowview	8	Dauphin	Winnipeg	Inwood	Bender Hamlet, Sat. 7.00
Windygates	6	Lisgar	W. & N., Lariviere		M. W. F. tr. 249.
Winkler	6	Lisgar	W. & N.		Dy. trs. 121, 122.
*Winnipeg		Winnipeg			
Winnipeg Beach	8	Selkirk	Winnipeg		Dy. tr. 235, C.P.R.

1 Closed via Gilbert Plains 1-12-14
2 Changed to Regent 1.4.15
3) Closed via Birtle

W
Z

OFFICE	KEY No.	COUNTY	DISTRIBUTION		

Office	Key No.	County	Distribution		
Winnipegosis.......	12	Dauphin......	{W. & S.A.......} {W. & H. ~~Jam~~} Dauphin......		T.T.S. tr. 3, via 137C.NR ~~M. W.~~ F. tr. 137. C.N.R.
Wood Bay.........	6	Lisgar.........	W. & N......		Dy. tr. 121.
Woodfield.........	8	Selkirk.......	Winnipeg......	St. Louis Guilbert........	M. W. SAT. 9.00.
Woodlands........	8	Macdonald.....	Winnipeg......		M.W.F. tr. 9, C.N.R.
Woodmore.........	8e	Provencher.....	B. L. & W.....	Dominion City	M.W.F. 8.00.
Woodnorth........	9a	Brandon......	B. & R.......		Dy. tr. 6, C.N.R.
Woodridge........	8a	Provencher....	~~Ft. F. & W.~~		~~Dy. trs. 21, 22.~~
Woodroyd........	8c	Selkirk.......	Winnipeg......	~~Stonewall~~	~~Thur. 7.30.~~
Woodside..........	3	P. la Prairie....	W. & Y........		M. W. F. trs. 57.
Woonona..........	8	Macdonald.....	Winnipeg......	Woodlands.....	Sat. 14.00.

OFFICE	KEY No.	COUNTY	DISTRIBUTION		
Zalicia		*Wpg & S.R. Garland*			*Sa. 14.0*

OFFICE	KEY No.	COUNTY	DISTRIBUTION		
Zant............	8	Dauphin.......	Winnipeg......	Ashern........	Sat. 7.00.
Zbaraz..........	8	Dauphin.......	Winnipeg......	Arborg........	Thu. 16.00.
Zhoda..........	8e	Provencher.....	{B. L. & W...} {E. & W......}	Emerson......	Vita, Sat. 11.30.
Zoria...........	12	Dauphin.......	W. & S. A.....	Sifton.........	Fri. 9.00.

Z

ALPHABETICAL LIST OF PLACES IN WESTERN ONTARIO SHOWING DESPATCH OF EACH FROM WINNIPEG STANDPOINT. THESE PLACES ARE KEYED TO THE FOLLOWING SIX SEPARATIONS:—

1.—Ft. Francis and Winnipeg R.P.O.
2.—Ft. William and Winnipeg R.P.O.
3.—Port Arthur.

4.—Fort William.
5.—Winnipeg District.
x2.—Sudbury L Ft. William.

NOTE.—Points in brackets ( ) are non-Post Offices.

Key No.	Office.	District.	Distribution.

ALPHABETICAL LIST OF PLACES IN WESTERN ONTARIO SHOWING DESPATCH OF EACH FROM WINNIPEG STANDPOINT. THESE PLACES ARE KEYED TO THE FOLLOWING SIX SEPARATIONS:—

1.—Ft. Francis and Winnipeg R.P.O.
2.—Ft. William and Winnipeg R.P.O.
3.—Port Arthur.

4.—Fort William.
5.—Winnipeg Dis.
x2.—Sudbury & Ft. William.

NOTE.—Points in brackets ( ) are non-Post Offices.

Key No.	Office.	District.	Distribution.
1	Atikokan	T. B. & R. R.	Ft. Francis. Pt. Arthur. Ft. William
x2	Aviemoor	Algoma	
1	Aylesworth	T. B. & R. R.	Emo.
4	Baird	T. B. & R. R.	
2	(Barclay Siding)		Bedworth
1	Banning	T. B. & R. R.	Ft. Francis Ft. William Pt. Arthur
1	Barnhart	T. B. & R. R.	Emo
1	Barwick	T. B. & R. R.	
1	(Bears Pass)		Ft. Francis
2	Bedworth	T. B. & R. R.	
2	(Begsley)		Tache Station
1	Bergland	T. B. & R. R.	Sleeman
1	Big Fork	T. B. & R. R.	Devlin
2	(Biota)		Savanne
x2	Biscotasing	Algoma	
1	Black Hawk	T. B. & R. R.	Barwick
2	Bonheur	T. B. & R. R.	
1	Boucherville	T. B. & R. R.	Stratton Stn.
1	Box Alder	T. B. & R. R.	Devlin
2	(Braid)		Ignace
2	(Brule Stn.)		Dinorwic
2	(Buda)		Kaministikwia
1	Burris	T. B. & R. R.	Devlin

ALPHABETICAL LIST OF PLACES IN WESTERN ONTARIO SHOWING DESPATCH OF EACH FROM WINNIPEG STANDPOINT. THESE PLACES ARE KEYED TO THE FOLLOWING SIX SEPARATIONS:—

1.—Ft. Francis and Winnipeg R.P.O.
2.—Ft. William and Winnipeg R.P.O.
3.—Port Arthur.

4.—Fort William.
5.—Winnipeg District.
x2.—Sudbury L Ft. William.

NOTE.—Points in brackets ( ) are non-Post Offices.

Key No.	Office.	District.	Distribution.
	Dearlock	Ft. F., W., Barwick, Black Hawk, Jne. 9 45	
(Summer Off.)	Cameron Island	Ft W & W, Kenora, Mon & Thur	
	Ellis	Ft Wm	M. W. F. Tu. 25
	Flanders	P/a. Form Ft Fra	

ALPHABETICAL LIST OF PLACES IN WESTERN ONTARIO SHOWING DESPATCH OF EACH FROM WINNIPEG STANDPOINT. THESE PLACES ARE KEYED TO THE FOLLOWING SIX SEPARATIONS:—

1.—Ft. Francis and Winnipeg R.P.O.
2.—Ft. William and Winnipeg R.P.O.
3.—Port Arthur.

4.—Fort William.
5.—Winnipeg Dis.
x2.—Sudbury & Ft. William

Note.—Points in brackets ( ) are non-Post Offices.

Key No.	Office.	District.	Distribution.
2	(Butler)		Ignace
1	(Calm Lake)		{Ft. Francis {Pt. Arthur
x2	Chapleau	Algoma	
1	Chapple	T. B. & R. R.	Barwick
3	Cloud Bay	T. B. & R. R.	
4 or 3	Conmee	T. B. & R. R.	
1	Crozier	T. B. & R. R.	
2	(Dagero)		
1	Dermid	T. B. & R. R.	Devlin
1	Devlin	T. B. & R. R.	
2	(Dexter)		
2	Dinorwic	T. B. & R. R.	
x2	Dorion Station	T. B. & R. R.	
2	Dryden	T. B. & R. R.	
2	Dyment	T. B. & R. R.	
2	Eagle River		Vermilion Bay
2	(Edison)		
1	Emo	T. B. & R. R.	
2	English	T. B. & R. R.	
x2	Everard	T. B. & R. R.	
2	(Falcon)		Ignace
3	Farrington	T. B. & R. R.	Port Arthur
1	Finland	T. B. & R. R.	Barwick
2	(Finmark)		Kaministikwia
3	Flint	T. B. & R. R.	

ALPHABETICAL LIST OF PLACES IN WESTERN ONTARIO SHOWING DESPATCH OF EACH FROM WINNIPEG STANDPOINT. THESE PLACES A█████ED TO THE FOLLOWING SIX SEPARATIONS:—

1.—Ft. Francis and Winnipeg R.P.O.
2.—Ft. William and Winnipeg R.P.O
3.—Port Arthur.

4.—Fort William.
5.—Winnipeg District.
x2.—Sudbury L Ft. William.

NOTE.—Points in brackets ( ) are non-Post Offices.

Key No.	Office.	District.	Distribution.

ALPHABETICAL LIST OF PLACES IN WESTERN ONTARIO SHOWING DESPATCH OF
EACH FROM WINNIPEG STANDPOINT. THESE PLACES ARE KEYED TO THE
FOLLOWING SEPARATIONS:—

1.—Ft. Francis and Winnipeg R.P.O.
2.—Ft. William and Winnipeg R.P.O.
3.—Port Arthur.

4.—Fort William.
5.—Winnipeg District.
x2.—Sudbury & Ft. William.

NOTE.—Points in brackets ( ) are non-Post Offices.

Key No.	Office.	District.	Distribution.
1	Fort Frances	T. B. & R. R.	
2	Fort William	T. B. & R. R....}	
2	Ft. William West	T. B. & R. R.	(Sub. Office of Ft. Wm.)
1	Gameland	T. B. & R. R.	Sleeman
2	(Guilbert)		Vermilion Bay
1	(Glenorchy)		Fort Frances
2	Gold Rock	T. B. & R. R.	Wabigoon
2	(Good Lake)		
4	(Grassey)		
2	(Gull River)		Ignace
2	Hawk Lake	T. B. & R. R.	
x2	Heron Bay	T. B. & R. R.	
3	(Huronian)		
3	Hymers	T. B. & R. R.	
2	Ignace	T. B. & R. R.	
2	Ingolf	T. B. & R. R.	
3	Intola	T. B. & R. R.	
1	Isherwood	T. B. & R. R.	Crozier.
x2	Jackfish	T. B. & R. R.	
1	Jual	T. B. & R. R.	Devlin.
3	Kakabeka Falls	T. B. & R. R.	Port Arthur. Ft. William. Ft. Frances.
2	(Kalmar)		
2	Kaministikwia	T. B. & R. R.	
1	Kashabowie	T. B. & R. R.	Ft. Frances. Pt. Arthur. Ft. William.

ALPHABETICAL LIST OF PLACES IN WESTERN ONTARIO SHOWING DESPATCH OF EACH FROM WINNIPEG STANDPOINT. THESE PLACES ARE KEYED TO THE FOLLOWING SIX SEPARATIONS:—

1.—Ft. Francis and Winnipeg R.P.O.
2.—Ft. William and Winnipeg R.P.O.
3.—Port Arthur.

4.—Fort William.
5.—Winnipeg District.
x2.—Sudbury L Ft. William.

NOTE.—Points in brackets ( ) are non-Post Offices.

Key No.	Offio	District.	Distribution.

ALPHABETICAL LIST OF PLACES IN WESTERN ONTARIO SHOWING DESPATCH OF EACH FROM WINNIPEG STANDPOINT. THESE PLACES ARE KEYED TO THE FOLLOWING SIX SEPARATIONS:—

1.—Ft. Frances and Winnipeg R.P.O.
2.—Ft. William and Winnipeg R.P.O.
3.—Port Arthur.

4.—Fort William.
5.—Winnipeg Dis.
x2.—Sudbury & Ft. William.

NOTE.—Points in brackets ( ) are non-Post Offices.

Key No.	Office.	District.	Distribution.
3	Kawene	T. B. & R. R.	
2	Keewatin	T. B. & R. R.	
2	Kenora	T. B. & R. R.	
3	Kivikoski	T. B. & R. R.	Port Arthur.
1	(Lac Seine)		Fort Frances.
4	(Lac Seul)		
1	Lake Wasaw	T. B. & R. R.	Devlin.
1	La Vallee	T. B. & R. R.	
1	(Little Grassey)		Sleeman.
1	(Long Sault)		Stratton Stn.
3	Mabella	T. B. & R. R.	
5	Malachi	T. B. & R. R.	
2	(Margach)		Vermilion Bay.
2	(Martin)		Bonheur.
5	McFarlane	T. B. & R. R.	
1	McInnes Creek	T. B. & R. R.	Rainy River.
5	McIntosh		
3	(Mattawin)		
1	(Matherford)		Emo.
2	Millar	T. B. & R. R.	
1	Minahico	T. B. & R. R.	Sleeman.
5	Minaki	T. B. & R. R.	
1	Mine Centre Station	T. B. & R. R.	Fr. Frances. Ft. William. Pt. Arthur.
2	Minnitaki	T. B. & R. R.	
x2	Missanabie	Algoma	

ALPHABETICAL LIST OF PLACES IN WESTERN ONTARIO SHOWING DESPATCH OF EACH FROM WINNIPEG STANDPOINT. THESE PLACES ARE KEYED TO THE FOLLOWING SIX SEPARATIONS:—

1.—Ft. Francis and Winnipeg R.P.O.
2.—Ft. William and Winnipeg R.P.O.
3.—Port Arthur.

4.—Fort William.
5.—Winnipeg District.
x2.—Sudbury *L* Ft. William.

NOTE.—Points in brackets ( ) are non-Post Offices.

Key No.	Office.	District.	Distribution.

ALPHABETICAL LIST OF PLACES IN WESTERN ONTARIO SHOWING DESPATCH OF EACH FROM WINNIPEG STANDPOINT. THESE PLACES ARE KEYED TO THE FOLLOWING SIX SEPARATIONS:—

1. Ft. Frances and Winnipeg R.P.O.
2.—Ft. William and Winnipeg R.P.O.
3.—Port Arthur.
4.—Fort William.
5.—Winnipeg Dis.
x2.—Sudbury & Ft. William.

NOTE.—Points in brackets ( ) are non-Post Offices.

Key No.	Office.	District.	Distribution.
3	Moose Hill	T. B. & R. R.	
1	Morson	T. B. & R. R.	Sleeman.
2	Murillo	T. B. & R. R.	
x2	Nemegos	Algoma	
x2	Nicholson Siding	Algoma	
x2	Nepigon	T. B. & R. R.	
2	(Niblock)		Savanne.
1	(Nickle Lake)		Fort Frances.
3	Nolalu	T. B. & R. R.	
2	Norman	T. B. & R. R.	
1	North Branch	T. B. & R. R.	Stratton. Stn.
4	(North East Bay)		
5 or 4	North Pines	T. B. & R. R.	
4	(O'Brien)		
3	O'Connor	T. B. & R. R.	
1	(Olive)		Ft. Frances.
2	(Osaquan)		Ignace.
x2	Ouimet	T. B. & R. R.	
2	Oxdrift	T. B. & R. R.	
2	(Parry)		Vermilion Bay.
1	Patullo	T. B. & R. R.	Stratton Stn.
x2	Pine	Algoma	
1	Pinewood	T. B. & R. R.	
2	(Poland)		Savanne.
2	Port Artour	T. B. & R. R.	
x2	Port Coldwell	T. B. & R. R.	

ALPHABETICAL LIST OF PLACES IN WESTERN ONTARIO SHOWING DESPATCH OF EACH FROM WINNIPEG STANDPOINT. THESE PLACES ARE KEYED TO THE FOLLOWING SIX SEPARATIONS:—

1.—Ft. Francis and Winnipeg R.P.O.
2.—Ft. William and Winnipeg R.P.O.
3.—Port Arthur.

4.—Fort William.
5.—Winnipeg District.
x2.—Sudbury L Ft. William.

NOTE.—Points in brackets ( ) are non-Post Offices.

Key No.	Office.	District.	Distribution.
4	Silver Islet (S.O.)		
3	Scoble West		Aymers M ‖ 12³⁰

ALPHABETICAL LIST OF PLACES IN WESTERN ONTARIO SHOWING DESPATCH OF
EACH FROM WINNIPEG STANDPOINT. THESE PLACES ARE KEYED TO THE
FOLLOWING SIX SEPARATIONS:—

1.—Ft. Francis and Winnipeg R.P.O.   4.—Fort William.
2.—Ft. William and Winnipeg R.P.O.   5.—Winnipeg Dis.
3.—Port Arthur.   x2.—Sudbury & Ft. William.

NOTE.—Points in brackets ( ) are non-Post Offices.

Key No.	Office.	District.	Distribution.
x2	Pulp Siding	Algoma	
5	Quibell	T. B. & R. R.	~~Vermilion Bay~~
1	Rainy River	T. B. & R. R.	
2	Raith	T. B. & R. R.	
2	(Raleigh)		Tache Station.
x2	Ramsay	Algoma	
1	Rapid River	T. B. & R. R.	Rainy River.
5 or 4	Richan	T. B. & R. R.	Sioux Lookout.
1	(Rocky Inlet)		Fort Frances.
3	Rosslyn Village	T. B. & R. R.	
x 2	Rossport	T. B. & R. R.	
x2	Ruel	Algoma	
4	St. Anthony Mine	T. B. & R. R.	Wabo Sat. 700
1	Sannes	T. B. & R. R.	Sleeman.
2	Savanne	T. B. & R. R.	
x2	Schreiber	T. B. & R. R.	
2	(Scovil)		Vermilion Bay.
3	Sellars	T. B. & R. R.	
3	(Shaboqua)		
2	(Sheba)		Savanne.
1	Shenston	T. B. & R. R.	Stratton Stn.
4 or 5	Sioux Lookout	T. B. & R. R.	
3	Silver Mountain	T. B. & R. R.	
3	Slate River Valley	T. B. & R. R.	
1	Sleeman	T. B. & R. R.	

ALPHABETICAL LIST OF PLACES IN WESTERN ONTARIO SHOWING DESPATCH OF
EACH FROM WINNIPEG STANDPOINT. THESE PLACES ARE KEYED TO THE
FOLLOWING SIX SEPARATIONS:—

1.—Ft. Francis and Winnipeg R.P.O.
2.—Ft. William and Winnipeg R.P.O.
3.—Port Arthur.

4.—Fort William.
5.—Winnipeg District.
x2.—Sudbury L Ft. William.

NOTE.—Points in brackets ( ) are non-Post Offices.

Key No.	Office.	District.	Distribution.

ALPHABETICAL LIST OF PLACES IN WESTERN ONTARIO SHOWING DESPATCH OF EACH FROM WINNIPEG STANDPOINT. THESE PLACES ARE KEYED TO THE FOLLOWING SIX SEPARATIONS:—

1.—Ft. Frances and Winnipeg R.P.O.
2.—Ft. William and Winnipeg R.P.O.
3.—Port Arthur.

4.—Fort William.
5.—Winnipeg Dis.
x2.—Sudbury & Ft. William.

NOTE.—Points in brackets ( ) are non-Post Offices.

Key No.	Office.	District.	Distribution.
2	(Snell).....................	....	Vermilion Bay.
3	South Gillies...............	T. B. & R. R...........	
3 or 4	Stanley......................	T. B. & R. R...........	
1	(Steep Rock)................	....	Fort Frances.
1	Stratton....................	T. B. & R. R...........	
4	Sturgeon Lake...............	T. B. & R. R...........	
4	Superior Junction...........	T. B. & R. R...........	
2	Tache Station...............	T. B. & R. R...........	
2	(Tamarac)...................	....	Bonheur.
x2	Trudeau.....................	T. B. & R. R...........	
1	(Turtle)....................	....	Fort Frances.
2	(Upsala)....................	....	Savanne.
2	Vermilion Bay...............	T. B. & R. R...........	
2	Wabigoon....................	T. B. & R. R...........	
5	(Wade)......................	....	
4	Wako.......................	T. B. & R. R...........	
2	Waldhof....................	T. B. & R. R...........	
3	Wamsley....................	T. B. & R. R...........	
x2	Wayland....................	Algoma................	
x2	White River................	T. B. & R. R...........	
x2	Windy Lake.................	Algoma................	
2	Winnipeg River Crossing).....	....